William Shakespeare's
HAMLET
adapted by
Michael Almereyda

faber and faber

To Manny Farber and Patricia Patterson

First published in 2000
by Faber and Faber Limited
3 Queen Square London WC1N 3AU
Published in the United States by Faber and Faber, Inc.,
an affiliate of Farrar, Straus and Giroux LLC, New York

Photoset by Parker Typesetting Service, Leicester
Printed in England by Mackays of Chatham PLC, Chatham, Kent

The Introduction first appeared, in slightly
altered form, in the *New York Times*.

A CIP record for this book
is available from the British Library

ISBN 0 – 571 – 20689–1

2 4 6 8 10 9 7 5 3 1

CONTENTS

FESTIVAL INTERNAZIONALE DEL FILM LOCARNO

ACCREDITATI

Michael
Almereyda

| 3 | 4 | 5 | 6 | 7 | 8 | 9 | 10 | 11 | 12 | 13 |

PREFACE

'If I feel physically as if the top of my head were taken off,' Emily
Dickinson once said, 'I know that is poetry.'

I'll get back to this, in a minute.

We were in the lobby of a midtown bank at three a.m., filming
that scene – you know the one – in which the ghost of Hamlet's
father (Sam Shepard) appears on a surveillance monitor,
prompting Hamlet's spooked pals to dash to the elevator to check
it out. After the second take, one of the producers turned to me
and said, 'This reminds me of Scooby-Doo.' I didn't feel insulted.
It wasn't the first or last time I had to face the implicit question:
What are we doing here? Why *Hamlet* – again – here and now?

The answer leads back to Emily Dickinson by way of Orson
Welles, who conjured up a version of *Macbeth* in 1948, shooting for
21 days on an RKO sound stage cluttered with fantastic, soggy-
looking papier-mâché sets. Welles described his film as 'a rough
charcoal sketch' of the play, and this remark, alongside the finished
picture, provoked in me a sharp suspicion that you don't need lavish
production values to make a Shakespeare movie that's accessible
and alive. Shakespeare's language, after all, is lavish enough. The
meaning and emotion are all embedded there, line for line, word for
word. In the last 400 years, who more than Shakespeare has been so
directly responsible for transmitting the particular electrical charge
that Emily Dickinson described – the recognition of sudden and
contrary meanings colliding in your brain, a certain top-of-your-
head-being-taken-off feeling? Dickinson herself felt the ceiling lift
when reading Shakespeare. After first taking in a volume of his plays,
she was prompted to ask: 'Why is any other book needed?'

At any rate, I was visited by an elemental desire to film
Shakespeare. It was, as Emily would have it, practically a physical
impulse – like wanting to go swimming in the ocean, or running
out into a storm at night. Then again, maybe it wasn't so purely
hedonistic. I had some hope that my reflexes as a film-maker
would be tested, battered and bettered. That I'd be swept along
into deeper Shakespearean currents.

I was hovering over various possibilities, relatively obscure plays – and I was resisting *Hamlet*. It seemed too familiar, too obvious, and it's been filmed at least 43 times. Better to leave it to high school productions, spoofs and skits and *The Lion King*. As T. S. Eliot noted years back, *Hamlet* is like the Mona Lisa, something so overexposed you can hardly stand to look at it.

But masterpieces are definably masterpieces because they have a way of manifesting themselves in our everyday lives. The play, and the character, seemed to be chasing me around New York. I passed high school kids quoting *Hamlet* on the street. I was informed of the existence of a *Hamlet* porno film ('To fuck or not to fuck . . .'). And I found myself thinking back to my first impressions of the play, remembering its adolescence-primed impact and meaning for me – the rampant parallels between the melancholy Dane and my many doomed and damaged heroes and imaginary friends: James Agee, Holden Caulfield, James Dean, Egon Schiele, Robert Johnson, Vladimir Mayakovsky, Jean Vigo.

I was struck by the fact that no film of *Hamlet* features a truly young man. In dozens of versions (including two silent films with women in the title role) none of the actors was under thirty, and the most definitive, conspicuous modern incarnations – Olivier, Richard Burton, Kevin Kline, Mel Gibson – were all at least forty when they tackled the part. (Kenneth Branagh, at thirty-five, seemed hardly any younger, despite his trim platinum haircut and the enthusiastic swashbuckling moves unleashed during the climactic duel.) Why not entrust the role to an actor in his twenties? The character takes on a different cast when seen more clearly as an abandoned son, a defiant brat, a narcissist, a poet/film-maker/perpetual grad student – a radiantly promising young man who doesn't quite know who he is. (The play's famously simple first line is 'Who's there?'.)

And I was heartened by the Polish scholar Jan Kott's passionately lucid 1964 book, *Shakespeare Our Contemporary*. 'The genius of *Hamlet*,' Kott wrote, 'consists in the fact that the play can serve as a mirror. An ideal *Hamlet* would be one most true to Shakespeare and most modern at the same time.'

Given the story's familiarity, it seemed altogether natural to locate a new *Hamlet* in the immediate present, to translate the Danish kingdom into a multimedia corporation, and to watch the story unfold in penthouse hotel rooms, sky-level office corridors, a coffee shop, an airplane, the Guggenheim Museum. The chief thing was to balance respect for the play with respect for contemporary reality – to see how thoroughly Shakespeare can speak to the present moment, how they can speak to each other.

When I showed Ethan Hawke a eight-page treatment and explained my intention – to shoot fast and cheap in New York, to film in super 16mm, to make everything as urgent and intimate as possible, keeping all spoken dialogue as written by Shakespeare but set within and energized by a contemporary context – Ethan got it immediately. He trusted me, and he was ready, with a breathtaking absence of Hamlet-like equivocation, to leap in. 'You know,' he said during our first discussion, in a bar, over mid-afternoon glasses of beer, 'we don't have to go to Yale to do this.' Then again, given 400 years of tradition, we knew we could never prepare enough.

Ethan worked with an actor who had previously played Hamlet on stage (a gifted man too modest and ambitious to want himself credited as a coach), and we met at least once a week, reading and talking through the play, most often in Ethan's study, where he tended to pace around the pool table that dominated the room.

Ethan's contributions were essential. Fortified by Harold Goddard's excellent critical study, *The Meaning of Shakespeare* (unfortunately out of print), he made a case for Hamlet as someone whose hesitation to kill Claudius is justified, contrary to the questionable imperatives of revenge or the bloodlust of an impatient audience. Hamlet doesn't need to kill Claudius, Ethan insisted, once he's made the man face his own guilt: 'There's nothing in the body of Shakespeare's work that suggests he thinks murder is a good thing.' The level of vulnerability Ethan brought to the role, the quality of imploding self-doubt, it tempered by this conclusion, as is our entire treatment of the story.

Later on, Ethan passed me a video cued to a clip of the Vietnamese monk Thich Nhat Hanh, whose concept of 'inter-being' felt like a perfect ramp leading up to Hamlet's most famous soliloquy. I tossed it into the mix. The one modern pre-recorded voice, I'd like to think, that Shakespeare wouldn't consider an intrusion.

Through all this I was watching every version of *Hamlet* available in New York, scheduling systematic visits to the Museum of Modern Art, the Museum of Television and Radio and the Library for the Performing Arts at Lincoln Center. (This is a curiously claustrophobic activity. You plug yourself into headphones and a monitor mounted within a tight Formica cubicle, surrounded almost exclusively by middle-aged men studying old Broadway musicals.)

Of course, I rummaged through books of critical theory but, more to the point, I never stopped reading the play, which carries the best advice for any director: 'Suit the action to the word, the word to the action.' This is so smart and simple it's almost stupefying.

The screenplay came together quickly and even easily – a process of channelling and distillation. (Typing Shakespeare straight into your computer is a thrilling act of ventriloquism that I can recommend to any writer.) My main job, anticipating work behind the camera, was to imagine a parallel visual language that might hold a candle to Shakespeare's poetry. There was no wish to illustrate the text, but to focus it, building a visual structure to accommodate Shakespeare's imagery and ideas.

From what I can tell, global corporate power is as smoothly treacherous and absolute as anything going in a well-oiled feudal kingdom, and the notion of an omnipresent Denmark Corp. provided an easy vehicle for Claudius's smiling villainy. But this was a key opening a wider door. It's more meaningful to explore how Shakespeare's massive interlocking themes – innocence and corruption, identity and fate, love and death, the division between thought and action – might be heightened, even clarified, when colliding with the spectacle of contemporary media-saturated technology.

Shakespeare, after all, has Hamlet caught in the wheels of his own hyperactive mind, enthralled by 'words words words'. The film admits that images currently keep pace with words, or outstrip them, creating a kind of overwhelming alternate reality. So nearly every scene in the script features a photograph, a TV monitor, an electronic recording device of some kind. The play-within-the-play becomes Hamlet's homemade video projection.

Polonius eavesdrops on his daughter by wiring a microphone to her shirt. (This was Ethan's inspiration, courtesy of Linda Tripp.) And while nature, in the dialogue, is continually invoked, the characters in the film are never exposed to a real landscape until they arrive, *en masse*, at Ophelia's funeral – the graveyard being the only respite from the city's hard surfaces, mirrors, screens and signs.

In reviews published since the movie's premiere, in late January at the Sundance Film Festival, the only criticism that's rattled me are the strangely bitter complaints about 'product placement' – carping fuelled by the cynical assumption that billboards and logos on display in the film were promotional throwaways by which the producers lined their pockets. The undignified, all but unbelievable truth is that we paid for the privilege of parading certain logos and insignias across the screen. There was, after all, an intended point. 'Denmark is a prison,' Hamlet declares early on, and if you consider this in terms of contemporary consumer culture, the bars of the cage are defined by advertising, by all the hectic distractions, brand names, announcements and ads that crowd our waking hours. And when, in this independent film, the ghost of Hamlet's father vanishes into a Pepsi machine, or Hamlet finds himself questioning the nature of existence in the 'Action' aisles of a Blockbuster video store, or Shakespeare's lines are overwhelmed by the roar of a plane passing overhead – it's meant as something more than casual irony. It's another way to touch the core of Hamlet's anguish, to recognize the frailty of spiritual values in a material world, and to get a whiff of something rotten in Denmark on the threshold of our self-congratulatory new century.

All the same, the film contains some dazzling contradictions. The fact that this *Hamlet*, skidding into being on a perilously low budget, happens to feature a notably high-profile cast – prominent actors all working for scale – is further testament to Shakespeare's supernatural status as the great leveller, unifier of mighty opposites.

In most cases, the actors were my first choices, and all of them were distinctly invested in their roles. Sam Shephard volunteered that he had a habit of reciting Hamlet's 'To be or not to be' soliloquy while driving in his truck, alone, on long cross-country trips. Once we were into it, preparing the ghost's big speech, he confided that he'd never worked so hard on a part, never felt so challenged. (I can report, in turn, that I never saw the ghost played with such an electrifying sense of reality.) Bill Murray, showing up for the script reading, disingenuously announced that nobody had ever asked him to play Shakespeare before. (He then confessed he'd taken workshops, years earlier, with the magical voice coach and scholar Kristin Linklater, and he handled the language with such eccentric agility that I'm hoping he tackles a heftier Shakespearean role down the road.) It also emerged that Mr Murray, in the course of an action-packed career, had never taken on a film in which he was obliged to die. Whereas Ethan Hawke had always resisted roles requiring his character to kill someone. And here we all were – all the actors in the film doing miraculous work, coerced by Shakespeare into facing an extended part of themselves, a new kind of reality.

It's a truism that every movie is made three times: in the writing, in the shooting, and in the editing, each process generating new contingencies and surprises. And so, many of our best and worst ideas fell by the wayside –sacrificed for the sake of clarity and momentum and to dodge mistakes, making this latest *Hamlet* the most condensed straight film adaptation in English. Entire scenes were dropped, Shakespeare's text was further trimmed and torn, and the result is, inevitably, an *attempt* at *Hamlet* – not so much a sketch but a collage, a patchwork of intuitions, images and ideas.

'Who's there?' The famous stark first line was finally cut, with great reluctance. But we never stopped asking ourselves the question. Shakespeare's most inexhaustible play – an echo chamber, a bottomless well, a hall of mirrors, an untamable beast – keeps throwing back infinite answers.

Michael Almereyda
May 2000

INTRODUCTION
Ethan Hawke

'Hamlet *is, without a doubt, the best play ever written, partly because it lends itself to so many changes and interpretations. The actor, however he plays it, well or badly, will get something right in his journey from the castle walls to his final silence.*'

Laurence Olivier

'I just don't see what's so marvelous about Sir Laurence Olivier, that's all. He has a terrific voice and he's a hell of a handsome guy and he's very nice to watch walking or duelling or something but . . . He was too much like a goddamn general instead of a sad screwed-up type guy.'

Holden Caulfield in *Catcher in the Rye* on seeing *Hamlet*

There is a lot of eye rolling that goes on whenever you tell someone you want to play *Hamlet* – 'What could *you* possibly have to offer?' The answer to me always was very simple – nothing. But the play itself has a tremendous amount to offer. It always does. Productions good or bad – there will always be something valuable and beautiful about listening to the language of an outrageous, maniacal, chop-your-head-off genius.

Over the years, too many productions of *Hamlet* have been focused on the central performance; the only thing that distinguished the movie or play was the actor in the title role. Conversely, in Michael Almereyda's first treatment outlining his idea for a new film of *Hamlet*, it seemed clear to me that he had an exciting, encompassing attack on the play as a whole – the only kind of production where I felt I could succeed. In my personal experience with the play I've always been dreadfully bored in that long fourth act where Hamlet does not appear – yawning my way through Ophelia's suicide – and I think it's a testament to the cohesiveness of Michael's vision that this section of the film is one of the most electric.

There were little things I had hopes of bringing to the role. Namely, feeling that at twenty-seven I was a little more appropriately cast than most. I've always thought that the reason

Hamlet comes off so annoying, infantile, and self-indulgent is that the guy playing him is ten to twenty years too old for the part. He is a bright young man struggling deeply with his identity, his moral code, his relationship to his parents and with his entire surrounding community. These are archetypal young man's concerns. Hamlet was always much more like Kurt Cobain or Holden Caulfield than Sir Laurence Olivier.

There was another idea that I'd hoped to articulate, which was to address some common criticisms of Hamlet: that he is cowardly or indecisive. Hamlet is decisive, he just also happens to be a thoughtful and decent human being who doesn't take lightly the idea of killing another human being. In fact, Hamlet's first instinct is not to kill the King but to set about proving his guilt with 'The Mousetrap'. Only slowly is his mind eroded by the desire to please a dead father to whom he was never close (there is much to suggest that Hamlet feared his father, but I can't imagine from the descriptions of 'Valiant' Hamlet Sr. that he and his theatre-loving son were tight). There is nothing in the play that suggests killing Claudius is a good or correct thing to do. Nothing but more death and the collapse of the kingdom is brought about by Hamlet's pursuit of his old man's vigilante challenge. Hamlet remains throughout the play a little unsettled as to whether what he saw was a 'spirit from Heaven or a goblin damned', and I think that you could build a good case that that Ghost breathed nothing but evil into his son's ear, that the play is the story of a father reaching out from beyond the grave and corrupting and burdening the mind of his child with the baggage of his own vengeful anger and lust for power. How many people feel lost and drowning under the weight of their parents' judging eye?

Lastly there is a visceral and intimate quality that I feel cinema can bring to Shakespeare that is too easily lost in stage productions. Filming, editing and shaping the play allow the actor to focus his or her interpretation while taking the time to savour each moment. As a performer my largest aspiration was not to over-act. The role of Hamlet seduces even excellent actors into acting up a big storm. I wanted to let the words do everything, and to let them flow out of me as simply and effortlessly as possible. Hamlet's own speech to the players (which sadly had to be cut from the film) is the perfect compass: 'Do not saw the air too much with your hand, thus, but use all gently, for in the very torrent, tempest and (as I may say) whirlwind of your passion you must acquire and beget a temperance that may give it smoothness.'

The shoot was fast and furious and I remember very little of it. Rehearsing my lines as I tried to lull my infant daughter back to sleep is a more tangible memory to me than any of the actual playing. I was always so tired, running around Manhattan trying to remember my lines, having fifteen minutes to get a certain speech right before the sun came up, only to move on to a larger speech half an hour later. I was often envious of people who had had the opportunity to play the role on stage solely because I was learning so much day by day that by the end I would've loved the chance for another try at the whole thing.

During shooting Michael had given me his pixelvision camera to goof around with and to record Hamlet's video diaries. It was a great way for me to get inside the character, as well as useful in the film. I gave Michael hours and hours of footage, keeping my costumes and shooting for at least four or five days after production had been completed. It was difficult for me to let go of the part.

My favourite memory, however, remains of the months before shooting began, when a friend of mine who was acting as my coach would come over and we would lounge around poring over the play for hours, watching old productions and reading out aloud. I felt an obligation to study the play as a whole, rather than simply Michael's adaptation. I wanted to fully understand the motivation behind each scene and also gain a deeper understanding of the play so that I could be a more useful ally to Michael in the distillation process of adapting this massive work of dramatic literature into a two-hour film. Reading in the quiet of my own room, the play became so fresh and so personal that I couldn't help but feel that no one else had been given the full manuscript before.

I am seriously indebted to the other cast members of the film: Sam Shepard, Diane Venora, Bill Murray, Kyle MacLachlan, Liev Shieber, Julia Stiles, Karl Geary and everybody else. The belief, passion and enthusiasm that they brought to the set was always infectious. It was clear that each person present was there for the simple love of the playing.

New York, 2000

A NOTE ON THE ADAPTATION

It should go without saying that a screenplay is no substitute for the experience of reading Shakespeare unfiltered and unabridged. While sharing essential vital organs, cell tissue and a patchy epidermal layer with Shakespeare's *Hamlet*, the following adaptation is a separate creature, a mutation – all the more so since there's been a fair bit of gene-splicing undertaken to fuse the shooting script (dated 11 September 1998) with developments on view in the completed movie.

For the most part, Shakespeare's dialogue has been left long, even when later compressed in the editing room. Stuff that was dropped or cut appears in brackets to signify its non-existence in the finished film; asterisks indicate notes at the back of the book, chronicling evolutionary upheavals as scenes were revised, rescued or lost forever. This extra material is included on the off-chance that readers might be intrigued to see how thoroughly a director can gut his own screenplay and still come up with a movie that's considered fairly full-bodied.

I'm indebted to my heroically resourceful producers, Amy Hobby and Andrew Fierberg of double A films. They launched and sustained the production on an extremely threadbare budget, routinely accomplishing miracles to serve the script. David Edelstein and Austin Pendleton, reviewing early drafts, provided valuable criticism and encouragement. And Kristina Boden, picture editor, presided over the film's protracted birth with ingenuity, care and a kind of passionate cool-headedness. We'd been working on the movie a long while when she turned to me one morning and announced, casually, 'Last night, for the first time in months, I didn't dream about *Hamlet*.'

M. A.

William Shakespeare's *Hamlet*

adapted by

Michael Almereyda

CAST AND CREW

MAIN CAST
HAMLET Ethan Hawke
CLAUDIUS Kyle MacLachlan
GHOST Sam Shepard
GERTRUDE Diane Venora
POLONIUS Bill Murray
LAERTES Liev Schreiber
OPHELIA Julia Stiles
HORATIO Karl Geary
ROSENCRANTZ Steve Zahn
GUILDENSTERN Dechen Thurman
MARCELLA Paula Malcomson
BERNARDO Rome Neal
PRIEST Robert Thurman
GRAVEDIGGER Jeffrey Wright
OSRIC Paul Bartel

MAIN CREW
Directed by Michael Almereyda
Based on the play Hamlet *by* William Shakespeare
Screen Adaptation by Michael Almereyda
Produced by Amy Hobby & Andrew Fierberg
Executive Producers Jason Blum & John Sloss
Line Producer Callum Greene
Original Music Carter Burwell
Cinematography John de Borman
Film Editing Kristina Boden
Production Design Gideon Ponte
Art Direction Jeanne Develle
Costume Design Marco Cattoretti & Luca Mosca
Additional Photography Jim Denault & Jon Herron
City and Sky Shots Jem Cohen
'Mousetrap' Animation Lewis Klahr
Stills Larry Riley

EXT. NEW YORK CITY: TIMES SQUARE — NIGHT

A near-hallucinatory spectacle: traffic, neon, noise.

Amidst surrounding electronic displays, the animated logo for the DENMARK CORPORATION flashes and whirls.

EXT. HOTEL — NIGHT

A sleek modern façade, doorman, revolving doors.

Lights swim across the hotel's identifying metal plaque:

HOTEL ELSINORE

*[INT. HOTEL ELSINORE; LOBBY/SURVEILLANCE DESK — NIGHT

VIDEO MONITOR: THE LOBBY

A cavernous space, in low light. There's a surge of static. The image seems to shiver.

We hear Bernardo's voice muttering off-screen.

> **BERNARDO**
>
> Who's there?

No answer.

Two figures appear, walking hand in hand, their joined shadows reflected on the marble floor.

ANGLE ON THE SECURITY DESK

Bernardo, the night watchman, sits stationed before a bank of surveillance monitors, eating take-out Thai food. He looks exhausted. Marcella approaches.

> **MARCELLA**
>
> Olla, Bernardo!

> BERNARDO
> *(startled)*

What, is Horatio there?

Horatio rounds the corner, lighting a cigarette.

> HORATIO

A piece of him.

> BERNARDO

Welcome, Horatio. Welcome, good Marcella –

> MARCELLA

Has this thing appeared again tonight?

> BERNARDO

I have seen nothing.

> MARCELLA

Horatio says 'tis but our fantasy
And will not let belief take hold of him.
Therefore I have entreated him along
With us to watch the minutes of the night,
That, if again this apparition come,
He may approve our eyes and speak to it.

> HORATIO

Tush, tush, 'twill not appear.

Bernardo gestures with his chopsticks.

> BERNARDO

Sit down awhile –

> MARCELLA
> *(noting the monitor)*

Break thee off. Look where it comes again!

ON THE MONITOR: HOTEL LOBBY

The picture wavers, a ghostly flicker, as Hamlet's Father strides into view, a tall figure, his back to us.

The figure exits one monitor – then enters another, fluttering in the video haze.

BERNARDO

In the same figure like the king that's dead.

Horatio leans in, squinting at the monitor as Bernardo moves out from behind the desk. Marcella yanks at Horatio's sleeve.

INT. HOTEL HALLWAY – NIGHT

Horatio and Marcella hurry after Bernardo. Horatio looks cautious, unconvinced.

They round the corner – and see the ghost standing by the elevator, eyes downcast, waiting. Marcella keeps her voice low.

MARCELLA

Thou art a scholar. Speak to it, Horatio.

BERNARDO

Looks 'a not like the king? Mark it, Horatio.

HORATIO

Most like. It harrows me with fear and wonder.

BERNARDO

It would be spoke to.

MARCELLA

Speak to it, Horatio.

The elevator opens and the ghost steps in, glancing up for a moment, meeting Horatio's eyes as the door slides shut.

As if released from a spell, Horatio, Marcella and Bernardo rush forward. Marcella slaps the elevator button. They watch numbers descend – then the adjacent elevator car opens and they all hop in.

INT. HOTEL BASEMENT – NIGHT

Horatio, Marcella and Bernardo emerge from the elevator, catching sight of the ghost as he disappears around a corner.

They give chase, passing a maid punching numbers into a pay phone.

They round the corner and see the ghost moving towards a soda machine at the corridor's end.

Horatio ventures closer, not quite trusting his eyes.

> HORATIO
> I'll cross it, though it blast me.
>> (*to the ghost*)
> Stay, illusion.
> If thou hast any sound or use of voice,
> Speak to me.
>> (*the ghost pauses*)
> What are thou that usurpst this time of night,
> Together with that fair and warlike form
> I' which the majesty of buried Denmark
> Did sometimes march?

No response. The ghost keeps his back to them.

> By heavens I charge thee speak!

> MARCELLA
> It is offended.

Horatio moves forward, his ire up.

> HORATIO
> If there be any good thing to be done,

8

That may to thee do ease and grace to me,
Speak to me!
If thou art privy to thy country's fate,
Which happily foreknowing may avoid,
O, speak!

The ghost steps closer to the soda machine – and seems to dissolve into the radiant façade.

Stay! Speak, speak! I charge thee, speak!

Horatio steps close to the machine, then turns back to his companions. Bernardo, in a sweat, looks particularly shaken.

This bodes some strange eruption to our state.

Marcella approaches the machine. She studies it a moment then slugs coins into the slot, punches a button. A can of Coke arrives with a thud; she hands it to Bernardo.

Let us impart what we have seen tonight
Unto young Hamlet; for upon my life,
This spirit, dumb to us, will speak to him.]

INT. CORPORATE CORRIDOR – DAY

Hamlet stands silhouetted before the New York skyline visible behind him through a wide window. His hair is unkempt, he's wearing a dark suit, and he's studying a portable video unit held in one hand.

ON VIDEO MONITOR

A news broadcast of Claudius, the King, speaking into banked microphones.

A squeal of feedback prompts Hamlet to reduce the volume. He switches to another channel – another image of Claudius.

                    KING
                 (*voice-over*)
Though yet of Hamlet our dear brother's death
The memory be green –

Hamlet switches to channel 3. The monitor now displays an image fed from a pixelvision video camera held in his other hand – a black-and-

white image of the corridor he's standing in. The corridor walls are
windows giving a view of surrounding buildings and sky.

Hamlet proceeds to walk down the hall, keeping the camera at chest
level. Off-screen, we hear Claudius's amplified, confident voice, growing
more distinct as Hamlet approaches.

(*voice-over*)
– And that it us befitted
To bear our heart in grief, and our whole kingdom
To be contracted in one brow of woe –

Hamlet rounds the corner, encountering a tall heavy bodyguard. The
bodyguard gives a look of recognition, and opens the door.

INT. CONFERENCE ROOM – DAY

Claudius speaks into microphones and a phalanx of cameras. He has
the focused, burnished look of a man accustomed to attention and
power. At his side sits Gertrude, his wife, early forties, Hamlet's mother.
Her dark eyes carry a quality of ravenous awareness.

KING
–Yet so far hath discretion fought with nature
That we with wisest sorrow think on him
Together with remembrance of ourselves . . .

He reaches for his wife's hand. Tears are welling in her eyes.

Close by sit Polonius, the King's adviser/spin doctor, and Polonius's
children Laertes and Ophelia. Laertes is wearing a suit and tie. Ophelia
is wearing a skirt and a cardigan over a T-shirt. Her face is luminous
and intensely watchful. In her hands is a small package wrapped in gold
paper.

She glances up, spotting Hamlet as he edges his way into the room. He
sits slouched on the window ledge, recording with his camera.

Therefore our sometime sister, now our Queen,
Th' imperial jointress to this warlike state –

Claudius keeps squeezing Gertrude's hand. A current of emotion seems
to be conducted in this touch.

Have we, as 'twere, with a defeated joy,
With an auspicious and a dropping eye,
With mirth in funeral, and with dirge in marriage,
In equal scale weighing delight and dole,
Taken to wife.

Gertrude kisses Claudius. Hamlet lowers his camera, shutting off the monitor. Ophelia sketches a picture of a waterfall on the gold packet, and keeps glancing at Hamlet.

Nor have we herein barred
Your better wisdoms, which have freely gone
With this affair along. For all –

Claudius pauses, and Gertrude completes the sentence.

QUEEN
– our thanks.

Polonius leads the applause, triggering a fusillade of flash bulbs. Claudius brings out a copy of Usa Today *and holds it up, indicating a photo of a scruffy young man with a terrorist's blank gaze, Fortinbras. The accompanying headline: FORTINBRAS MAKES BID ON DENMARK CORP.*

KING
Now follows that you know young Fortinbras
Holding a weak supposal of our worth,
Or thinking by our late dear brother's death
Our state to be disjoint and out of frame –

Ophelia nudges Laertes, indicating that he should pass her packet to Hamlet. Laertes narrows his eyes, refusing.

Polonius, noting the exchange, does not look pleased.

Co-leagued with this dream of his advantage,
He hath not failed to pester us with message
Importing the surrender of those lands
Lost by his father, and with all bond of law,
To our most valiant brother.

With a big smile and a flourish, Claudius rips the newspaper in two.

So much for him.

INT. HALLWAY LINKING SKYSCRAPERS — DAY

Claudius makes his way down the corridor. Laertes and Polonius keep pace with him. Hamlet hangs back, escorting his mother.

> KING
> And now Laertes, what's the news with you?
> The head is not more native to the heart,
> The hand more instrumental to the mouth,
> Than is the throne of Denmark to thy father.
> What would'st thou have, Laertes?

Over this Ophelia approaches Hamlet, passing him her gold-wrapped packet. Laertes, turning to Claudius, distractedly takes note of them.

> LAERTES
> My dread Lord,
> Your leave and favour to return to France,
> From whence, though willingly I came to Denmark
> To show my duty in your coronation,
> Yet now I must confess, that duty done,
> My thoughts and wishes bend again to France.

> KING
> Have you your father's leave? What says Polonius?

> POLONIUS
> He has, my lord, wrung from me my slow leave
> By laboursome petition, and at last
> Upon his will I sealed my hard consent.
> I do beseech you give him leave to go.

Over this, Laertes takes a few quick sideways steps and pulls Ophelia away from Hamlet.

> KING
> Take thy fair hour, Laertes. Time be thine.
> And thy best grace spend it at thy will.

Gertrude takes Hamlet's arm, steering him to the door – but Hamlet impetuously returns to Ophelia, delivering a quick kiss.

*Hamlet walks ahead of Gertrude, Claudius and an ever-present
bodyguard, surrounded by mid-town skyscrapers. Hamlet's withdrawn,
shut down.*

KING

Cousin Hamlet, and my son –
How is it that the clouds still hang on you?

Hamlet doesn't answer. Gertrude glides up, taking his arm.

QUEEN

Good Hamlet, cast thy nighted colour off,
And let thine eye look like a friend on Denmark.
Do not forever with thy vailed lids
Seek for thy noble father in the dust.
Thou know'st 'tis common; all that lives must die,
Passing through nature to eternity.

HAMLET

Ay, madam, it is common.

QUEEN

If it be,
Why seems it so particular with thee?

He pauses, as if unable to breath, forcing himself to look at her.

HAMLET

Seems, madam? Nay, it is; I know not 'seems'.
'Tis not alone my inky cloak, good mother,
Nor customary suits of solemn black,
Nor windy suspiration of forced breath,
No, nor the fruitful river in the eye,
Nor the dejected havior of the visage,
Together with all forms, moods, shapes of grief,
That can denote me truly. These indeed seem,
For they are actions that a man might play.
But I have that within which passes show;
These but the trappings and the suits of woe.

Gertrude crosses to the waiting limo as Claudius firmly takes Hamlet's arm.

'Tis sweet and commendable in your nature, Hamlet,
To give these mourning duties to your father.
That father lost, lost his, and the survivor bound
In filial obligation for some term
To do obsequious sorrow. But to persevere
In obdurate condolement is a course
Of impious stubbornness. 'Tis unmanly grief.
It shows a will most incorrect to heaven,
A heart unfortified, a mind impatient.

The limo window slides down, and Gertrude, removing her glasses, speaks to her son.

QUEEN
Let not thy mother lose her prayers, Hamlet.
I pray thee stay with us, go not to Wittenberg.

Hamlet wants to roar a dozen questions, but instead he says, quietly:

HAMLET
I shall in all my best obey you, madam.

[EXT. HOTEL — DAY

Wind buffets passing pedestrians.

INT. HOTEL LOBBY — DAY

Hamlet hurries past the surveillance desk without giving Bernardo a second look.

INT. HOTEL HALLWAY — DAY

Hamlet inserts his key-card, opens the door.]

INT. HAMLET'S HOTEL SUITE, BACK ROOM — DAY

Hamlet sits at a desk rewinding tape on his clamshell monitor.

Ophelia's unwrapped gift is close at hand: a heart-shaped cookie glazed and patterned with miniature candy hearts.

The bed has been shoved near one wide window. Books, magazines, videotapes and CDs are scattered everywhere. On the wall: a collage-like array of postcards, photos and clippings.

Hamlet speaks quietly, his attention focused on the monitor.

                    HAMLET
O that this too too solid flesh would melt,
Thaw, and resolve itself into a dew
Or that the everlasting had not fixed
His canon 'gainst self slaughter.

[Now (and throughout the rest of this soliloquy) we FLASH CUT to glimpses of Hamlet's immediate memory. Hamlet's voice occasionally spills over these cuts, but the bulk of the soliloquy is to be played on camera.

EXT. DENMARK CORPORATION – DAY

Claudius joins Gertrude in the waiting limousine, leaving Hamlet alone on the sidewalk.

EXT. SIDEWALK (NEAR FOUNTAIN) – DAY

Hamlet runs up a flight of steps, stumbles, stops, ties his shoe. Pedestrian traffic swarms around him.]

INT. HAMLET'S BACK ROOM – DAY

                    HAMLET
Oh God, God,
How weary, stale, flat and unprofitable
Seem to me all the uses of this world!
Fie on't, ah, fie, 'tis an unweeded garden
That grows to seed. Things rank and gross in nature
Possess it merely.

[EXT. FOUNTAIN – DAY

Hamlet kisses Ophelia, softly, tenderly, uncomfortably. The fountain is thundering behind them. Ophelia is cold, shivering; Hamlet opens his eyes.]

HAMLET

That it should come to this:
But two months dead, nay, not so much, not two –

Hamlet presses PLAY, reviewing pixel footage of his mother and father ice skating. They embrace, stumble, regain their footing, hug and laugh.

So excellent a king, that was to this
Hyperion to a satyr, so loving to my mother
That he might not beteem the winds of heaven
Visit her face too roughly.

ON THE MONITOR

A series of shots of Ophelia on ice. She's unsteady but radiant, gliding.

An abrupt cut, and we see Ophelia in bed, her face obscured by a book. She lifts the book, glances at the camera, then turns away.

Hamlet rewinds then freezes the image, then he stands, moves to a shelf, fits a CD in his Discman.

HAMLET

Heaven and earth
Must I remember? Why, she would hang on him
As if increase of appetite had grown
By what it fed on; and yet within a month –
Let me not think on't; frailty, thy name is woman –
A little month, or ere these shoes were old
With which she followed my poor father's body
Like Niobe, all tears, why she, even she –

Brahm's First Symphony booms from brick-sized speakers as Hamlet moves to the terrace, which is spectacularly framed on three sides by a grid of skyscraper windows.

O god, a beast that wants discourse of reason
Would have mourned longer – married with my uncle,
My father's brother but no more like my father
Than I to Hercules, within a month,
Ere yet the salt of most unrighteous tears
Had left the flushing in her galled eyes,

She married. Oh most wicked speed, to post
With such dexterity to incestuous sheets!
It is not, nor can it come to good.
But break, my heart, for I must hold my tongue –

The doorbell buzzes. Hamlet, a bit rattled, shuts off the video monitor, then bounds into the front room.

INT. HAMLET'S FRONT ROOM – DAY

[*Hamlet crosses to the door, opens it. There stand Horatio, Marcella and Bernardo.*

HORATIO
Hail to your lordship!

Hamlet lets them in. Their talk rides on a current of deadpan sarcasm.

HAMLET
I am glad to see you well,
Horatio – or I do forget myself.

HORATIO
The same, my lord, and your poor servant ever.

HAMLET
Sir, my good friend, I'll change that name with you.]

Horatio drops onto the couch, and Marcella collapses close beside him. Bernardo, still on the job, stands awkwardly hovering.

And what make you from Wittenberg, Horatio?
Marcella?

She leans into Horatio, fumbling in his jacket pocket for a cigarette.

MARCELLA
My good lord.

HAMLET
I am very glad to see you.
         (*to Bernardo*)
Good even, sir.
         (*back to Horatio*)
But what, in faith, make you from Wittenberg?

HORATIO
A truant disposition, good my lord.

HAMLET
But what is your affair in Elsinore?
We'll teach you to drink deep ere you depart.

Horatio lights cigarettes for Marcella and himself.

HORATIO
My lord, I came to see your father's funeral.

Hamlet clicks off the music, leaving them in abrupt silence.

HAMLET
I prithee, do not mock me, fellow student,
I think it was to see my mother's wedding.

HORATIO
Indeed, my lord, it followed hard upon.

HAMLET
Thrift, thrift, Horatio. The funeral baked meats
Did coldly furnish forth the marriage tables.

A trilling sound. Reaching into his pocket, Horatio brings out a ringing beeper. He promptly shuts if off.

Would I have met my dearest foe in heaven
Or ever I had seen that day, Horatio!
My father! – Methinks I see my father –

And now Horatio's face darkens.

HORATIO
Where, my lord?

HAMLET
In my mind's eye, Horatio.

HORATIO
I saw him once. He was a goodly king.

HAMLET
He was a man, take him for all in all,
I shall not look upon his like again.

HORATIO
My lord, I think I saw him yesternight.

HAMLET
Saw? Who?

HORATIO
My lord, the king, your father.

HAMLET
The king my father?

Horatio stands, looking for an ashtray as he proceeds to talk.

HORATIO
Season your admiration for a while
With an attent ear till I may deliver
Upon the witness of this gentleman
        (*indicating Bernardo*)
This marvel to you.
        (*he crosses back to Hamlet*)
In the dead waste and middle of the night
The apparition comes. I knew your father;
These hands are not more like.

HAMLET

But where was this?

MARCELLA

My lord, upon the platform where we watched.

HAMLET

Did you not speak to it?

HORATIO

My lord, I did,
But answer made it none.
Yet once methought it lifted up its head and did address
Itself to motion, like as it would speak.
But even then – it shrunk in haste away
And vanished from our sight.

Hamlet sits beside Marcella.

HAMLET

'Tis very strange.

HORATIO

As I do live, my honoured lord, 'tis true,
And we did think it writ down in our duty
To let you know of it.

HAMLET

Indeed, indeed, sir. But this troubles me.
                    (*to Bernardo*)
Hold you the watch tonight?

BERNARDO

I do, my lord.

HAMLET

What looked he, frowningly?

HORATIO

A countenance more in sorrow than in anger.

HAMLET

And fixed his eyes upon you?

HORATIO

Most constantly.

HAMLET

I would that I had been there.

HORATIO

It would have much amazed you.

Hamlet sees that Marcella's been eyeing a room service tray of half-eaten french fries. He gestures for her to dig in; she does so.

HAMLET

I will watch tonight.

Horatio nods approval.

I'll speak to it though hell itself should gape
And bid me hold my peace. I pray you all,
If you have hitherto concealed this sight,
Let it be tenable in your silence still,
And whatsoever else shall hap tonight,
Give it an understanding but no tongue.
I will require your loves. So fare you well –

He leads them to the door. Handshakes and hugs.

Upon the platform, 'twixt eleven and twelve,
I'll visit you.

BERNARDO

Our duty to your honour.

HAMLET

Your loves, as mine to you.
Farewell.

He shuts the door after them. And now deep concern and sadness shadow his face. He moves to the window.

Would the night were come.
Till then sit still my soul.
Foul deeds will rise,
Though all the earth o'erwhelm them, to men's eyes.

Ophelia is looking at a photo of young Hamlet, a fourteen-year-old holding a still camera. Her brother is close beside her. They're in their father's multi-levelled apartment, surrounded by books, glass and lucite surfaces, a wide view of the East River.

LAERTES

For Hamlet, and the trifling of his favour,
A violet in the youth of primy nature,
Forward, not permanent, sweet, not lasting,
The perfume and suppliance of a minute,
No more.

OPHELIA

No more but so?

LAERTES

Think it no more,
For nature crescent does not grow alone
In thews and bulk, but as this temple waxes,
The inward service of the mind and soul
Grows wide withal. Perhaps he loves you now,
And now no soil nor cautel doth besmirch

The virtue of his will; but you must fear,
His greatness weighed, his will is not his own.
For he himself is subject to his birth.

Ophelia stands, irked, only half listening as Laertes continues.

He may not, as unvalued persons do,
Carve for himself; for on his choice depends
The safety and health of this whole state;
And therefore must his choice be circumscribed
Unto the voice and yielding of that body
Whereof he is the head. Then if he says he loves you,
It fits your wisdom so far to believe it
As he in his particular act and place
May give his saying deed, which is no further
Than the main voice of Denmark goes withal.

Ophelia sits again, gathering photos in a little box.

Then weigh what loss your honour may sustain
If with too credent ear you list his songs,
Or lose your heart, or your chaste treasure open
To his unmastered importunity.

*She looks at him, not quite able to suppress her surprise. He touches her
hand.*

Fear it, Ophelia, fear it, my dear sister,
And keep you in the rear of your affection,
Out of the shot and danger of desire.
Best safety lies in fear;
Youth to itself rebels, though none else near.

OPHELIA
I shall the effect of this good lesson keep
As watchman to my heart, but, good my brother,
Do not, as some ungracious pastors do,
Show me the steep and thorny way to heaven,
While like a puffed and reckless libertine
Himself the primrose path of dalliance treads
And recks not his own rede.

His air of seriousness dissolves. He forces a laugh. We hear an elevator whirr and click.

Ophelia and Laertes both look up, glimpsing their father's feet crossing a transparent overhead walkway.

LAERTES

O, fear me not.
I stay too long.
A double blessing is a double grace;
Occasion smiles upon a second leave.

Polonius makes his way down the stairs.

POLONIUS

Yet here, Laertes? Aboard, aboard, for shame!
The wind sits in the shoulder of your sail
And you are stayed for.

Laertes and Ophelia both stand. They seem a bit afraid of their father. Laertes heads downstairs; Polonius follows.

My blessing with thee –
And these few precepts in thy memory
Look thou character.

Ophelia watches as the men move away from her.

INT. POLONIUS'S APARTMENT – DAY

Polonius joins Laertes in the apartment's lower level and proceeds to help him pack, all the while rattling through his inventory of 'precepts'.

POLONIUS

Give thy thoughts no tongue,
Nor any unproportioned thought his act.
Be thou familiar, but by no means vulgar.
Those friends thou hast, and their adoption tried,
Grapple them to thy soul with hoops of steel,
But do not dull thy palm with entertainment
Of each new-hatched, unfledged comrade.
Beware of entrance to a quarrel, but being in,
Bear't, that th' opposed may beware of thee.

Laertes is impatient, scarcely listening, preoccupied with his luggage.

> Give every man thy ear, but few thy voice;
> Take each man's censure, but reserve thy judgement.
> Costly thy habit as thy purse can buy,
> But not expressed in fancy; rich, not gaudy,
> For the apparel oft proclaims the man.
> Neither a borrower nor a lender be,
> For loan oft loses both itself and friend.

Father and son stand facing each other now, a stark, stilted moment. Polonius reaches into himself for some final advice.

> This above all: to thine own self be true,
> And it must follow, as the night the day,
> Thou canst not then be false to any man.

They embrace, awkwardly. Then Laertes pulls away.

LAERTES
Most humbly do I take my leave, my lord.

POLONIUS
The time invites you. Go.

Laertes heads for the door with suitcases weighing him down – and encounters Ophelia, poised at the foot of the stairs. He embraces her and, reaching into her hair, removes a small butterfly-shaped hair pin.

LAERTES
Farewell, Ophelia, and remember well
What I have said to you.

[INT. APARTMENT ELEVATOR – DAY

The elevator descends, carrying Laertes, suddenly alone with himself, preoccupied.

INT. HAMLET'S BACK ROOM – NIGHT

Hamlet moves to the window, reviewing footage on his pixel monitor. Bits of plastic and paper are blowing around on the terrace.]

EXT. MID-TOWN MANHATTAN – NIGHT

A limousine cuts through traffic.

INT. LIMOUSINE – NIGHT

Claudius and Gertrude, elegantly dressed, are sharing a newspaper whose front page shows a photo of Claudius tearing up yesterday's newspaper. The headline: DENMARK THWARTS FORTINBRAS. Claudius has his hand on Gertrude's leg and is leaning close, whispering into her ear.

Hamlet sits across from them, seething as the limo slows.

EXT. MOVIE THEATRE – NIGHT

The limo door opens and Gertrude and Claudius get out, greeted by photographers and onlookers crowded behind velvet ropes. We're at a major movie premiere.

Hamlet follows the King and Queen as photographers shout, flash bulbs pop. Gertrude and Claudius are in their element, smiling graciously as they move into the theatre.

But Hamlet veers off, cuts through the crowd, running from the event.

INT. HOTEL ELSINORE, LOBBY/SURVEILLANCE DESK – NIGHT

Bernardo studies the surveillance monitor with Horatio and Marcella beside him. Bernardo glances at his watch, then reaches for the phone.

INT. HAMLET'S FRONT ROOM – NIGHT

The TV is on without sound. The phone starts ringing – but Hamlet lies curled on the couch, asleep with his clothes on.

Then he sits up – and slowly reacts. His father's ghost is standing on the terrace, staring straight at him

Hamlet stares back, and a strange calm overtakes him. He moves to the adjoining room.

INT. HAMLET'S BACK ROOM – NIGHT

Hamlet heads for the terrace door while the ghost, immobile, waits for him. The window shows Hamlet's reflection advancing amidst a constellation of city lights.

HAMLET

Angels and ministers of grace defend us!
Be thou a spirit of health or goblin damned,
Bring with thee airs from heaven or blasts from hell,
Be thy intents wicked or charitable
Thou coms't in such a questionable shape
That I will speak to thee.

Hamlet opens the door, and the ghost steps in . . .

Hamlet closes the door, shutting out city noise as the ghost surveys the disordered room. On the soundless TV, men are trying to extinguish roaring flames.

Hamlet Sr faces his son. They both look awkward and sad, registering a kind of mutual disappointment.

GHOST

Mark me.

HAMLET

I will.

GHOST

My hour is almost come
When I to sulphrous and tormenting flames
Must render up myself.

HAMLET

Alas, poor ghost!

GHOST

Pity me not, but lend thy serious hearing
To what I shall unfold.

HAMLET

Speak. I am bound to hear.

The ghost brings his handkerchief to his ear, then moves toward Hamlet.

GHOST

I am thy father's spirit,
Doomed for a certain term to walk the night,
And for the day confined to fast in fires,
Till the foul crimes done in my days of nature
Are burnt and purged away. But that I am forbid
To tell the secrets of my prison house,
I could a tale unfold whose lightest word
Would harrow up thy soul, freeze thy young blood,
Make thy two eyes like stars start from their spheres,
Thy knotted and combined locks to part
And each particular hair stand on end
Like quills upon the fearful porpentine.
But this eternal blazon must not be
To ears of flesh and blood. List, list, O, list!
If thou did'st ever thy dear father love –

*The ghost steps close and, speaking with intense urgency, touches
Hamlet's hair, his face, his chest.*

HAMLET

O God!

GHOST

Revenge his foul and most unnatural murder.

Hamlet pulls away.

HAMLET

Murder?

GHOST

Murder most foul, as in the best it is,
But this most foul, strange and unnatural.

*Hamlet withdraws, trying to get a hold of himself, but the ghost follows,
moving deeper into the room.*

Now, Hamlet, hear.
'Tis given out that, sleeping in my orchard,
A serpent stung me. So the whole ear of Denmark
Is by a forged process of my death
Rankly abused. But know, thou noble youth,

The serpent that did sting thy father's life
Now wears his crown.

HAMLET

My uncle!

He says it as if this is what he's expected, what he knows.

GHOST

Ay, that incestuous, that adulterate beast,
With witchcraft of his wits, with traitorous gifts –
O wicked wit and gifts, that have the power
So to seduce! – won to his shameful lust
The will of my most seeming-virtuous queen.

*Hamlet looks heartsick, amazed and appalled. His father, we might
sense, never spoke to him so directly while alive.*

Oh Hamlet, what a falling-off was there,
From me, whose love was of that dignity
That it went hand in hand even with the vow
I made to her in marriage, and to decline
Upon a wretch whose natural gifts were poor
To those of mine.
– But soft, methinks I scent the morning air.

*The ghost freezes, abruptly cautious, staring out into the night like a
vampire fearing daylight.*

Brief let me be. Sleeping within my orchard,
My custom always of the afternoon,
Upon my secure hour thy uncle stole
With juice of cursed hebona in a vial,
And in the porches of my ears did pour
The leprous distillment, whose effect
Holds such an enmity with blood of man
That swift as quicksilver it courses through
The natural gates and alleys of the body,
And with a sudden vigour it doth posset
And curd, like eager droppings into milk,
The thin and wholesome blood. So did it mine.

The ghost turns back to Hamlet.

31

Thus was I, sleeping, by a brother's hand
Of life, of crown, of queen, at once dispatched,
Cut off even in the blossoms of my sin
Unhouseled, disappointed, unaneled,
No reck'ning made, but sent to my account
With all my imperfections on my head.
O, horrible! O, horrible, most horrible!
If thou hast nature in thee, bear it not.

He turns away, moving towards the terrace door.

Let not the royal bed of Denmark be
A couch for luxury and damned incest.
But, howsoever thou pursues this act,
Taint not thy mind, nor let thy soul contrive
Against thy mother aught. Leave her to heaven
And to those thorns that in her bosom lodge
To prick and sting her. Fare thee well at once . . .

He abruptly returns and embraces his son, whispering fiercely in his ear.

Remember me.

Hamlet is suddenly alone in his room. Facing the wall of windows, the silent flame-filled TV. Badly shaken and confused.

HAMLET

My fate cries out –

The doorbell buzzes.

[INT. HAMLET'S FRONT ROOM – NIGHT

Hamlet hurries to the door, flings it open – revealing Horatio and Marcella, looking somewhat put out. They enter the room. Hamlet just looks stunned.

HORATIO

My lord . . .

Marcella flops into the couch, whistling to get Hamlet's attention.

MARCELLA

Illo, ho, ho, my lord.

HORATIO

What news, my lord?

Hamlet looks at them, perplexed. Then chooses to be circumspect, attempting casualness and talking fast. But he can't quite conceal his agitation.

HAMLET

It is an honest ghost, that let me tell you.
For your desire to know what is between us,
O'ermaster 't as you may.
     (ignoring their disappointed looks)
And now, good friends,
Give me one poor request.

HORATIO

What is't, my lord? We will.

HAMLET

Never make known what you have seen tonight.

Horatio and Marcella look at each other. What have they seen?

Nay but swear 't.

HORATIO

Propose the oath, my lord.

HAMLET

Never to speak of this that you have seen.

Marcella and Horatio remain mystified.

MARCELLA

These are but wild and whirling words, my lord.

HAMLET

I am sorry they offend you.

HORATIO

There's no offence, my lord.

HAMLET

But there is, Horatio,
And much offence too.

33

Horatio remains puzzled. Marcella feels a chill and, noting her discomfort, Horatio crosses to the open window – glancing out at the terrace.]

Hamlet moves beside Horatio as they both see the ghost, Hamlet Sr, standing on the ledge, his back to us, as if contemplating a fatal leap. Then he glances over at Hamlet.

Horatio gasps and drops his cigarette – and the ghost vanishes.

HORATIO
O day and night, but this is wondrous strange!

Marcella scuffs out Horatio's cigarette, then joins them at the window. She's confused – has seen nothing. Hamlet faces Horatio with fresh resolve.

HAMLET
And therefore as a stranger give it welcome.
There are more things in heaven and earth, Horatio,
Than are dreamt of in our philosophy.
[But come; here, as before –

He shuts the window. Horatio and Marcella step near.

Never, so help you mercy,
How strange or odd soe'er I bear myself,
As I perchance hereafter shall think meet
To put an antic disposition on –
That you, at such times seeing me, never shall,
With arms encumbered thus, or this headshake,
Or by pronouncing of some doubtful phrase
Or such ambiguous giving out, to note
That you know aught to me: this do swear.
So grace and mercy at your most need help you.

HORATIO AND MARCELLA
My Lord, we will.

Hamlet glances back at the window.

HAMLET
(*voice-over*)
Rest, rest, perturbèd spirit.

34

(*turning back to Horatio and Marcella*)
And still your fingers on your lips, I pray.]

EXT. NEW YORK SKYLINE – DAWN

Buildings seem to thaw in the morning light. We hear the electronic squalling of an Internet connection riding a surflike sound of white noise.

HAMLET
(*voice-over*)
The time is out of joint. O cursèd spite
That ever I was born to set it right!

INT. POLONIUS'S APARTMENT – DAY

Ophelia taps numbers into the telephone. A hectic pre-recorded voice responds.

MR MOVIEFONE
(*voice-over*)
Hello and welcome to Moviefone, sponsored by *The New York Times* and 102.7, WNEW . . . If you know the name of the movie you'd like to see, press one now –

Over this, Polonius coasts up behind her, hovers a moment, then clicks off the phone.

POLONIUS
What is't, Ophelia, he hath said to you?

OPHELIA
So please you, something touching the Lord Hamlet.

She stands, withdrawing to a ledge overlooking the river. Polonius follows, sits beside her.

POLONIUS
Marry, well bethought.
What is between you? Give me up the truth.

OPHELIA
He hath, my lord, of late made many tenders
Of his affection to me.

35

POLONIUS

Affection! Think yourself a baby
That you have ta'en these tenders for true pay
Which are not sterling. Tender yourself more dearly.

OPHELIA

My lord, he hath importuned me with love in honourable
fashion.

POLONIUS

When the blood burns, how prodigal the soul
Lends the tongue vows.

*Ophelia has taken hold of a curious diorama – a glass-fronted box
featuring a view of a gravel road disappearing into a dim forest glade.
Her hand hovers over the glass.*

These blazes, daughter,
Giving more light than heat, extinct in both,
Even in their promise, as it is a-making,
You must not take for fire.

Polonius, impatient, wrests the box out of her hands.

From this time
Be something scanter of your maiden presence.
Set your entreatments at a higher rate
Than a command to parley. For Lord Hamlet,
Believe so much in him that he is young
And with a larger tether may he walk
Than may be given you.

She looks up at him, sternly, as if to challenge this.

Do not believe his vows, for they are brokers,
Not of that dye which their investments show,
But mere implorators of unholy suits.
I would not, in plain terms, from this time forth
Have you so slander any moment leisure
As to give words or talk with the Lord Hamlet.

*His voice is heated but, over this, he grabs Ophelia's foot and ties her
unlaced sneaker. Then he stands.*

Look to't, I charge you. Come your ways.

She looks after him, conflicting thoughts ricocheting in her head.

INT. HAMLET'S BACK ROOM – DAY

Thich Nhat Hanh speaks from a bedside TV.

> THICH NHAT HANH
> We have the word 'to be', but what I propose is the word 'to inter-be'. Because it's not possible to be alone, to be by yourself. You need other people in order to be.

Hamlet, holding the clam-shell monitor, crosses to his unmade bed.

> Not only do you need mother, father, but also uncle, brother, sister, society. But you also need sunshine, river, air, trees, birds, elephants and so on.

Hamlet studies the monitor: a repeated pixel image of Ophelia in bed, a book covering her face. She lifts the book, looks into the camera.

> So it is impossible to be alone. You have to inter-be with everyone and everything else. And therefore 'to be' means 'to inter-be'.

[*Hamlet pulls himself out of bed, crosses to a book shelf – and finds the book Ophelia had been reading.*

EXT. TERRACE – DAY

Hamlet drifts out to the railing with the open book. He pages through it but can't seem to concentrate.

Wind ruffles his hair, stirs the book's pages.

He stares out at surrounding buildings. And deliberately drops the book – pages fluttering as it falls.

Hamlet leaves the terrace, then returns with an armload of books. He proceeds to toss them into the air, one after another. They flutter open and fall like shot birds.

After a moment, the hotel phone starts to ring.]

INT. COFFEE SHOP – NIGHT

Hamlet's in a booth, hunched over a copybook and a cup of coffee. He starts to write, then tears and crumples the page. Starts again.

> HAMLET
> (*voice-over*)
To the celestial, and my soul's idol, the most beautified Ophelia . . .

He looks up.

[*Bernardo approaches and sits at Hamlet's table. Reaching into his jacket, Bernardo pulls out a folded plastic Strand Books bag. He passes the bag to Hamlet.*

Hamlet tentatively reaches into the bag. We glimpse a handgun wrapped in a T-shirt.

He stands and embraces Bernardo.]

EXT. KEY FOOD – NIGHT

Hamlet walks past derelicts standing outside the store. He keeps walking.

HAMLET
(*voice-over*)

Doubt thou the stars are fire,
Doubt that the sun doth move –

He turns, walking back in the direction he's just travelled. Then he decisively crosses the street.

(*voice-over*)

Doubt truth to be a liar –

EXT. SQUAT – NIGHT

Hamlet arrives outside a rundown building. The façade looks scarred and scorched.

HAMLET
(*voice-over*)

But never doubt I love.

Among the index of names on the mailbox, 'Ophelia' is spelled out in spidery handwriting.

A curtained area, an improvised dark room. On the walls: thrift store paintings, colour xeroxes and a virtual mural of Polaroid photos: a grid of flowers and weeds. Ophelia, wearing a tanktop and dungarees, is hanging wet prints on a clothesline. She looks phantasmal in the red safety light.

She turns, startled, as Hamlet slips into the room. He ducks under hanging prints and moves close.

She looks at him with a kind of clouded tenderness as he proceeds to unfold the thing in his hand – a square of painfully folded paper. The poem from the coffee shop.

He takes Ophelia's wrist, staring into her eyes as he presses the paper into her hand.

She unfolds the letter, reads.

[Hamlet reaches into his jacket and pulls out the bag Bernardo handed to him. He unwraps the T-shirt and extracts the gun, staring at it as if trying to imagine what it's doing in his hand. Then, looking up, he gives a start –

There's a man in the connected back room, sitting on the edge of the bed. It's Polonius, looking at Hamlet with cold, imperious hatred. Hamlet looks back to Ophelia – and now sees that the prints hanging overhead are portraits of her father.

Hamlet backs away, gun in hand.

His letter drops to the floor.

Ophelia stares after him, shocked, as he staggers out the door.

And Polonius emerges from the other room, looking pointedly at Ophelia.

POLONIUS

– Mad for thy love?

She kneels and picks up Hamlet's letter.

OPHELIA

My Lord, I do not know,
But truly I do fear it.]

40

Polonius takes the letter from Ophelia. She looks at him a moment, then lets go, looking particularly vulnerable.

She moves to the window.

HER POV:

Hamlet half-jogs across the street.

INT. HAMLET'S BACK ROOM – NIGHT

Hamlet sits at his editing desk, facing a TV wired to his clamshell monitor. The monitor displays a pixel close-up of Hamlet's face, blankly staring into the camera. He brings his gun to his temple, then lowers it. The image is running in reverse.

> HAMLET
> (*on monitor; in reverse*)
>
> To be or not to be . . .
> (*clears his throat, starts again*)
> To be or not to be . . .

FADE OUT.

FADE IN:

EXT. DENMARK CORPORATION – DAY

The sky looks like wax.

INT. DENMARK CORPORATION ELEVATOR – DAY

CLOSE ON HAMLET'S CLAMSHELL MONITOR.

Hamlet, in a previously recorded pixel close up, mutters into the camera.

> HAMLET
> (*on monitor*)
> So oft it chances in particular men,
> That for some vicious mole of nature in them,
> As in their birth, wherein they are not guilty –

The elevator opens. Hamlet gets out, carrying his monitor, which continues playing. He pauses at the window.

> (*on monitor*)
> By the o'ergrowth of some complexion,
> Oft breaking down the pales and forts of reason.
> Or by some habit that too much o'erleavens
> The form of plausive manners, that these men,
> Carrying, I say, the stamp of one defect,
> Being nature's livery or fortune's star,
> Their virtues else, be they as pure as grace,
> Shall in the general censure take corruption
> From that particular fault –

Midway over the above, Polonius glides up.

> POLONIUS
> How does my good Lord Hamlet?

Hamlet looks up. His eyes are opaque, walled off from the world. He quickly shuts off the monitor, folds it up.

> HAMLET
> Well, God-a-mercy.

> POLONIUS
> Do you know me, my lord?

HAMLET
Excellent well. You are a fishmonger.

Hamlet continues down the hall; Polonius follows.

POLONIUS
Not I, my lord.

HAMLET
Then I would you were so honest a man.

POLONIUS
Honest, my lord?

HAMLET
Ay Sir. To be honest, as this world goes –

INT. DENMARK CORPORATION SURVEILLANCE MONITOR – DAY

HAMLET
(on monitor)
– Is to be one man picked out of ten thousand.

POLONIUS
(on monitor)
That's very true, my lord.

INT. CORPORATION HALLWAY – DAY

HAMLET
For if the sun breed maggots in a dead dog, being a good kissing carrion – Have you a daughter?

POLONIUS
I have, my lord.

Hamlet resumes walking.

HAMLET
Let her not walk i' the sun. Conception is a blessing, but as your daughter may conceive, friend, look to't.

Polonius pauses, then turns, staring up at the surveillance camera.

> POLONIUS
> (*on monitor*)

How say you by that? Still harping on my daughter. He is far gone. – And truly in my youth I suffered much for love.

ANGLE ON HAMLET

He pulls the handgun from his camera bag, keeping it concealed, close at his side, as Polonius re-approaches.

> POLONIUS

– Will you walk out into the air, my lord?

> HAMLET

Into my grave.

Hamlet resumes walking. Polonius follows, nonplussed.

> POLONIUS

My honourable lord, I will most humbly take my leave of you.

Hamlet glances back at him, pausing at the end of the hall.

> HAMLET

You cannot take from me anything that I will more willingly part withal – except my life –

He rounds the corner.

INT. CORPORATE OFFICE SPACE – DAY

In slow motion, Hamlet strides past cubicles and office personnel. Gathering momentum, he brings out his gun.

> HAMLET
> (*voice-over*)

Except my life . . .

He hurries past a startled receptionist, then grabs at the door to an inner office –

> (*voice-over*)

Except my life –

INT. CLAUDIUS'S OFFICE – DAY

Hamlet bursts into the room. His arm swings wide to cover any sudden movement – but the office is empty.

Hamlet, crestfallen, lowers the gun.

INT. THE KING'S POOL – DAY

Claudius is swimming laps.

Polonius walks in with Ophelia at his side.

There's an awkward moment as he splits his attention between Claudius, swimming, and Gertrude sitting poolside. She's in a tailored suit, eating a Danish and working on a laptop computer.

> POLONIUS
> My liege, and madam – To expostulate
> What majesty should be, what duty is,
> Why day is day, night night, and time is time,
> Were nothing but to waste night, day, and time.
> Therefore, since brevity is the soul of wit,
> And tediousness the limbs and outward flourishes –

As Claudius emerges from the pool, Gertrude tosses him a towel. He sits beside her; she helps towel him dry.

> I will be brief. Your noble son is mad.
> Mad call I it, for, to define true madness,
> What is't but to be nothing else but mad?
> But let that go.

> QUEEN
> More matter, with less art.

> POLONIUS
> Madam, I swear I use no art at all.
> That he is mad, 'tis true, 'tis true 'tis pity,
> And pity 'tis 'tis true – a foolish figure.
> But farewell it, for I will use no art.

Polonius reveals Hamlet's letter, sheathed in plastic.

Mad let us grant him, then, and now remains
That we find out the cause of this effect,
Or rather say, the cause of this defect
For this effect defective comes by cause.
Thus it remains, and the remainder thus.
Perpend;
I have a daughter – have while she is mine –
Who in her duty and obedience, mark,
Hath given me this. Now gather and surmise.

He hands Hamlet's letter to Claudius. Gertrude promptly snatches the letter from him. Gives it a quick once-over.

QUEEN
Came this from Hamlet to her?

Ophelia attempts to take back the letter, but Gertrude won't let go. Polonius steps in, firmly takes the letter, reads its last lines.

POLONIUS
'. . . Thine evermore, most dear lady, whilst this machine is to him, Hamlet.'

Ophelia, ashamed, humiliated, moves to the pool's deep end, looking down at her refracting reflection.

This in obedience hath my daughter shown me,
And more above, hath his solicitings,
As they fell out by time, by means, and place,
All given to mine ear.

KING
But how hath she received his love?

POLONIUS
What do you think of me?

KING
As of a man faithful and honourable.

POLONIUS
I would fain prove so. But what might you think
When I had seen this hot love on the wing –

47

As I perceived it, I must tell you that,
Before my daughter told me – what might you,
Or my dear Majesty your queen here, think,
If I had looked upon this love with idle sight?

Camera centres on Ophelia, still gazing into the pool.

What might you think? No, I went round to work,
And my young mistress thus I did bespeak:
'Lord Hamlet is a prince out of thy star.
This must not be.'

Ophelia jumps into the pool, crashing into the water, fully dressed.

JUMP CUT:

*Ophelia blinks. She's still standing by the pool. The jump occurred only
in her mind. Polonius continues talking.*

– She took the fruits of my advice
And he, repelled, a short tale to make,
Fell into a sadness, then into a fast,
Thence to a watch, thence into a weakness,
Thence to a lightness, and by this declension
Into the madness wherein now he raves,
And all we mourn for.

*Ophelia turns and crosses back to the adults. She takes Hamlet's letter
from the lounge chair where Gertrude has left it. Gertrude warily
watches her.*

KING

Do you think this?

QUEEN

It may be, very like.

POLONIUS
(*pointing to his head and shoulder*)
Take this from this, if this be otherwise.
If circumstances lead me, I will find
Where truth is hid, though it were hid indeed
Within the centre.

*[INT. CAB – NIGHT

The cab jostles forward, Hamlet looking agitated as Joe Torre's automated voice plays over the speaker.

> JOE TORRE
> (*voice-over*)
> You know, New York has the best of everything, from baseball teams to cab drivers. That doesn't mean you shouldn't play it safe –

Hamlet squints and leans forward in his seat.

Ahead of the cab, a woman on a bicycle is gliding past other vehicles. Looks like Ophelia. She's moving fast, her head covered by a safety helmet.

The cab stalls. Hamlet stares after the cyclist's retreating helmet.

He leans his head against the window and shuts his eyes. The cab jolts forward, city lights swimming by.

When Hamlet opens his eyes, Ophelia is right beside him, like a fulfilled wish, a dream. Her face is in profile, alert to traffic but not noticing him.

He sits back in the cab as she glances towards him/us. The cab slows; Ophelia spurts ahead.

EXT. KEY FOOD – NIGHT

The cab pulls to the kerb; Hamlet hurries out.

He takes a few rapid steps towards the squat, then stops himself.

He turns and walks away, buttoning his coat.

INT. WHITNEY MUSEUM – DAY

Hamlet approaches a large, mirrored, rotating screen in a darkened room. A quiet pre-recorded voice recites an on-going chant.

> VOICE
> (*voice-over*)
> . . . The one who conceals
> The one who chokes

49

The one who relies
The one who finds
The one who meets
The one who waits
The one who dives . . .

Hamlet stares at his reflection as images surge across the screen and, reflected, travel across the room's walls. Then his own voice mingles with the recorded chant.]

HAMLET
To be or not to be, that is the question:
Whether 'tis nobler in the mind to suffer
The slings and arrows of outrageous fortune,
Or to take arms against a sea of troubles,
And by opposing end them. To die, to sleep –
No more – and by a sleep to say we end
The heartache and the thousand natural shocks
That flesh is heir to.

Hamlet stops following the mirror, letting his reflection slide away, consumed in video flame.

'Tis a consummation
Devoutly to be wished. To die, to sleep . . .

INT. BLOCKBUSTER VIDEO – DUSK

Hamlet roams the bright aisles while an action movie plays on mounted monitors. Stentorian music and the sounds of explosions seem to follow him around the store.

HAMLET
(*voice-over*)
To sleep, perchance to dream. Ay, there's the rub,
For in that sleep of death what dreams may come
When we have shuffled off this mortal coil,
Must give us pause. There's the respect
That makes calamity of so long life.

Hamlet approaches the check-out counter with a load of tapes. Voice-over continues in a rush as the clerk rings them up.

(*voice-over*)
For who would bear the whips and scorns of time,
The oppressor's wrong, the proud man's contumely,
The pangs of disprized love, the law's delay
The insolence of office, and the spurns
That patient merit of th' unworthy takes.
When he himself might his quietus make
With a bare bodkin?

INT. HAMLET'S BACK ROOM – NIGHT

*Hamlet proceeds to edit images from disparate sources: we glimpse a
porn movie with Elizabethan costumes, and snippets from a silent film
'Hamlet'.*

HAMLET
Who would fardels bear,
To grunt and sweat under a weary life,
But that the dread of something after death,
The undiscovered country from whose bourn
No traveller returns, puzzles the will,
And makes us rather bear those ills we have
Than fly to others that we know not of?

Juxtaposed images of sex and death constitute the main action for the rest of the soliloquy.

> Thus conscience does make cowards of us all,
> And thus the native hue of resolution
> Is sicklied o'er with the pale cast of thought.
> And enterprises of great pitch and moment
> With this regard their currents turn awry
> And lose the name of action.

INT. BAR – NIGHT

Hamlet sits drinking as the DJ spins a record. Music pulses and pounds.

Two near-identical young men appear at Hamlet's side. Rosencrantz and Guildenstern. They hover expectantly. It takes a moment for Hamlet to notice them.

HAMLET
My excellent good friends! How dost thou, Guildenstern? Ah, Rosencrantz! Good lads, how do you both?

ROSENCRANTZ
As the indifferent children of the earth.

GUILDENSTERN
Happy in that we are not overhappy. On fortune's cap we are not the very button.

HAMLET
Nor the soles of her shoes?

ROSENCRANTZ
Neither, my lord.

Hamlet stands, unsteadily, and moves with them to the back of the bar, jostling past shadow figures, dancers and drinkers.

Hamlet tries to hold himself together, settling at a corner table. Rosencrantz and Guildenstern flank him and sit drinking, taking in the music, excited, expectant.

HAMLET
What news?

ROSENCRANTZ

None, my lord, but that the world's grown honest.

HAMLET

Then is doomsday near. But your news is not true. Let me
question more in particular. What have you, my good friends,
deserved at the hands of Fortune that she sends you to prison
hither?

GUILDENSTERN

Prison, my lord?

HAMLET

Denmark's a prison.

ROSENCRANTZ

Then is the world one.

HAMLET

A goodly one, in which there are many confines, wards, and
dungeons. Denmark being one o' the worst.

The music seems to intensify.

ROSENCRANTZ

We think not so, my lord.

HAMLET

Why, then, 'tis none to you, for there is nothing either good
or bad but thinking makes it so. To me it is a prison.

ROSENCRANTZ

Why, then your ambition makes it one.
'Tis too narrow for your mind.

*Hamlet stands, feeling suddenly, desperately trapped. He glances around
the bar. Everyone looks insidious and unreal.*

HAMLET

Oh God, I could be bounded in a nutshell and count myself a
king of infinite space, were it not that I have bad dreams. –
What make you here?

ROSENCRANTZ

To visit you, my lord, no other occasion.

Hamlet moves down the street, followed and then joined by Rosencrantz and Guildenstern. Hamlet looks furtive, furious. When he finally speaks, his voice is soft and low.

HAMLET

Were you not sent for? Is it a free visitation? Come, come, deal justly with me. Come, come. Nay, speak.

GUILDENSTERN

What should we say, my lord?

HAMLET

But to the purpose. You were sent for, and there is a kind of confession in your looks. I know the good King and Queen have sent for you.

They've arrived before a Nail Salon. The place is closed but the window's neon sign is still on, bathing their faces in bright green light.

ROSENCRANTZ

To what end, my lord?

HAMLET

That you must teach me. Be even and direct with me,
whether you were sent for or no.

Rosencrantz and Guildenstern exchange looks.

GUILDENSTERN

My lord, we were sent for.

*Hamlet faces them, searching their eyes. Light rain begins to fall.
Hamlet turns himself towards the parlour window.*

HAMLET

I will tell you why, so shall my anticipation prevent your
discovery, and your secrecy to the King and Queen moult no
feather.

*Almost simultaneously, Rosencrantz and Guildenstern open umbrellas,
protectively standing by as Hamlet stares in through the rain-flecked
window.*

I have of late, but wherefore I know not, lost all my mirth,
forgone all custom of exercises; and indeed it goes so heavily
with my disposition that this goodly frame, the earth, seems
to me a sterile promontory –

HAMLET'S POV: NAIL SALON (SLOW MOTION)

*A seven-year-old girl sits in one of the salon chairs, blowing soap
bubbles, waiting as her father mops the floor.*

HAMLET

– this most excellent canopy, the air, look you, this brave
o'erhanging firmament, this majestical roof fretted with
golden fire, why it appeareth nothing to me but a foul and
pestilent congregation of vapours.

*Now rain is sluicing over the window, obscuring the view. Hamlet
turns back to Rosencrantz and Guildenstern. He doesn't seem to see
them.*

What a piece of work is a man, how noble in reason, how
infinite in faculties, in action how like an angel, in
apprehension how like a god: the beauty of the world, the

paragon of animals, and yet to me, what is this quintessence of dust?

He abruptly breaks off, looking hard at his companions, as if trying to recognize them. Then his face relaxes, as if to erase and deflect all thought.

Gentlemen, you are welcome.
> (*but they're uncertain, wary*)

You are welcome, but my uncle-father and aunt-mother are deceived.

GUILDENSTERN

In what?

HAMLET

I am but mad north-northwest: when the wind is southerly I know a hawk from a handsaw.

The rain has relaxed. Hamlet looks away, glances up at the clearing sky, then back to Rosencrantz and Guildenstern.

My good friends.]

INT. KING AND QUEEN'S ROOM — NIGHT

Gertrude lies in bed, staring at Claudius sitting on the edge of the bed, talking into a speakerphone.

CLAUDIUS

And can you by no drift of conference
Get from him why he puts on this confusion,
Grating so harshly all his days of quiet
With turbulent and dangerous lunacy?

ROSENCRANTZ
> (*over phone*)

He does confess he feels himself distracted
But from what cause he will by no means speak.

Gertrude sits up, wrapping her legs around Claudius as she proceeds to unbutton his shirt.

GUILDENSTERN
(over phone)

Nor do we find him forward to be sounded
But with a crafty madness keeps aloof
When we would bring him on to some confession
Of his true state.

Gertrude leans into the speakerphone.

QUEEN

Did he receive you well?

GUILDENSTERN
(over phone)

Most like a gentleman.

ROSENCRANTZ
(over phone)

But with much forcing of his disposition.

GUILDENSTERN
(over phone)

Niggard of question, but of our demands
Most free in his reply.

Claudius momentarily breaks off from kissing Gertrude.

KING

Thank you Rosencrantz and gentle Guildenstern.

QUEEN

Thank you Guildenstern and gentle Rosencrantz.

GUILDENSTERN

We lay our service freely at your feet –

Claudius resumes kissing his wife, breaking off the phone connection as he rolls onto her receptive body.

INT. HAMLET'S BACK ROOM – DAY

Hamlet is in bed, alone with a plate of room service food, watching TV without sound: images of James Dean, suffering beautifully in East of Eden.

(*voice-over*)

O what a rogue and peasant slave am I.
Is it not monstrous that this player here,
But in a fiction, in a dream of passion
Could force his soul so to his own conceit
That from her working all his visage wanned,
Tears in his eyes, distraction in his aspect,
A broken voice, and his whole function suiting
With forms to his conceit? And all for nothing!

He shoves the tray off the bed, moves closer to the TV.

What would he do
Had he the motive and the cue for passion
That I have?

Hamlet takes his pixelvision rig and starts taping images off TV. James Dean arguing with his father.

Bloody bawdy villain.
Remorseless, treacherous, lecherous, kindless villain.

The pixel images – enlarging video scan lines and flutter – are ghostly and distorted.

Why, what an ass am I. This is most brave,
That I, the son of a dear father murdered,
Prompted to my revenge by heaven and hell,
Must, like a whore, unpack my heart with words
And fall a-cursing like a very drab.

He sets down the camera and tumbles out of bed.

He moves to the window, looking out onto the empty terrace. Then he returns to the TV, an idea taking shape in his head.

I have heard that guilty creatures sitting at a play
Have by the very cunning of the scene
Been struck so to the soul that presently
They have proclaimed their malefactions.
For murder, though it have no tongue, will speak
With most miraculous organ.

He picks up the camera, training it on the clamshell screen. What results is a sort of visual feedback, a flaring comet-like shape that begins to spiral in on itself.

> I know my course. The spirit that I have seen
> May be a devil, and the devil hath power
> T'assume a pleasing shape, yea, and perhaps
> Out of my weakness and my melancholy,
> As he is very potent with such spirits,
> Abuses me to damn me. I'll have grounds
> More relative than this. The play's the thing
> Wherein I'll catch the conscience of the king.

INT. THE KING'S OFFICE – DAY

CLOSE ON CARD

An announcement. The crowded, computer-generated text reads:

> *The Mousetrap* a film/video by Hamlet
> Prince of Denmark 8 PM the screening room

Claudius turns the card over, exchanges looks with Gertrude.

POLONIUS
'Tis most true, and he beseeched me to entreat your majesties
To hear and see the matter.

Polonius is kneeling beside Ophelia, taping a wire to her exposed waist. Ophelia stares over her father's head, looking at nothing. She's trying not to cry, but can't help herself.

KING
With all my heart, and it doth much content me
To hear him so inclined.

Turning to his speakerphone, he starts speaking almost instantly.

> Good gentlemen, give him a further edge
> And drive his purpose into these delights.

ROSENCRANTZ AND GUILDENSTERN
(*over phone*)
We shall, my lord.

Polonius adjusts a little microphone rigged near his daughter's shirt collar. Ophelia looks up, wiping her eyes as Gertrude speaks.

> QUEEN
> And for your part, Ophelia, I do wish
> That your good beauties be the happy cause
> Of Hamlet's wildness. So shall I hope your virtues
> Will bring him to his wonted way again.

Ophelia holds herself still, watchful, her mind racing.

EXT. UPTOWN NEW YORK – DAY

Mid-afternoon. Dark low sky. Pedestrians look furtive, fearful.

INT. HAMLET'S HOTEL ROOM – DAY

POV THROUGH PEEPHOLE: OPHELIA

She's wearing the wired shirt. In her hands: a small red box with a spiral design. She looks beautiful and miserable.

> HAMLET
> The fair Ophelia!

He opens the door and lets her in – then jabs his head out into the hall, as if to catch sight of someone spying.

Seeing nothing, he leads her into the front room. Books and papers still litter the floor. Ophelia steps around them.

> Nymph, in thy orisons
> Be all my sins remembered.

She sits down, uncertain.

> OPHELIA
> Good my lord,
> How does your honour these many a day?

> HAMLET
> I humbly thank you. Well, well, well.

He goes to the mini-bar, brings out two beers.

OPHELIA

My lord, I have remembrances of yours
That I have longèd long to redeliver.
I pray you now, receive them.

She proceeds to unload the box – a stack of letters, envelopes – and a little rubber duck. Despite its comical toy aspect, the object seems imbued with immense personal value. Hamlet resistantly stares at her.

HAMLET

No, not I,
I never gave you aught.

OPHELIA

My honoured lord, you know right well you did,
And with them words of so sweet breath composed
As made these things more rich. Their perfume lost,
Take these again, for to the noble mind
Rich gifts wax poor when givers prove unkind.
There, my lord.

He takes in the letters. In his eyes, an avalanche of hurt feeling. He turns away, then looks back at her.

HAMLET

Are you honest?

OPHELIA

My lord?

HAMLET

Are you fair?

OPHELIA

What means your lordship?

HAMLET

I did love you once.

OPHELIA

Indeed, my lord, you made me believe so.

HAMLET

You should not have believed me. I loved you not.

OPHELIA

I was the more deceived.

She's trying not to cry, and looks so wounded, innocent and young that Hamlet melts, moves towards her. He touches her cheek, his voice low and quiet.

HAMLET

Get thee to a nunnery. Why wouldst thou be a breeder of sinners?

He tries to kiss her, she turns away. He touches her shoulder; she turns into him, kisses him back.

I am myself indifferent honest, but yet I could accuse me of such things that it were better my mother had not borne me: I am very proud, revengeful, ambitious, with more offences at my beck than I have thoughts to put them in, imagination to give them shape, or time to act them in. What should such fellows as I do crawling between earth and heaven? We are arrant knaves all; believe none of us.

They're now kissing passionately. Hamlet's hand travels down her side, and under her shirt – she jerks away as his hand discovers the wire . . .

63

He detaches the small microphone. They stare at each other. A kind of shared shock. Then, Hamlet whispers:

Where's your father?

Ophelia can't answer; he speaks loudly, directly into the microphone.

Let the doors be shut upon him, that he may play the fool nowhere but in's own house!

He flings the microphone with a sweep of his arm, knocking beer bottles off the table, then he stands and leaves the room.

Get thee to a nunnery –

Ophelia sits there a moment, guilty and stricken. Then she reaches into her clothes, tears at the wire, rips off the battery belt. Frantically, fighting tears, she gathers up her letters and rubber duck and runs for the door.

EXT. STREET – DUSK

Ophelia on her bicycle, pumping through traffic, moving very fast.

INT. SQUAT – NIGHT

Ophelia enters, sets down her book bag. She looks wrecked.

She arrives at her flashing answering machine. Presses 'PLAY'.

Hamlet's enraged voice comes over the machine.

HAMLET
(*off-screen*)
If thou dost marry, I'll give thee this plague for thy dowry: be thou as chaste as ice, as pure as snow, thou shalt not escape calumny. Get thee to a nunnery. Go, farewell!

Ophelia stands listening, frozen, as the voice continues, rising in volume, ranting. She turns away, helpless, clutching at her hair.

(*off-screen*)
Or if thou wilt needs marry, marry a fool, for wise men know well enough what monsters you make of them. To a nunnery, go, and quickly too. Farewell. God hath given you one face,

and you make yourselves another. You jig and amble, and
you lisp; you nickname God's creatures –

*[Ophelia kneels beside the machine, picks it up, then smashes it
against the wall.]*

INT. PRIVATE SCREENING ROOM LOBBY – NIGHT

*Hamlet stands with Horatio before the screening room entrance as an
audience trickles in – upper-class, middle-aged men and women.
Hamlet is anxious, speaking rapidly while trying to remain calm.*

HAMLET
– Give me that man
That is not passion's slave, and I will wear him
In my heart's core, ay in my heart of heart,
As I do thee. Something too much of this . . .
Tonight, one scene comes near the circumstance
Which I have told thee, of my father's death.
I prithee, when thou seest that act afoot,
Observe my uncle. If his occulted guilt
Do not itself unkennel in one speech,
It is a damned ghost that we have seen.
Give him heedful note,
For I mine eyes will rivet to his face,
And after we will both our judgements join
In censure of his seeming.

HORATIO
Well, my lord –

*He breaks off, seeing Ophelia [arrive with Polonius. Ophelia passes
Hamlet without speaking to him, but Polonius hesitates.*

HAMLET
My Lord, you played once i' the University, you say?

POLONIUS
That did I, my Lord, and was accounted a good actor.

HAMLET
What did you enact?

I did enact Julius Caesar. I was killed i' th' Capitol. Brutus killed me.

HAMLET

It was a brute part of him to kill so capital a calf there.

Aiming a finger at Polonius, Hamlet mimes a gunshot. Staggering into the theatre, Polonius pantomimes his death.]

Hamlet turns back to Horatio.

Get you a place. I must be idle.

INT. PRIVATE SCREENING ROOM — NIGHT

Polonius joins Claudius and Gertrude near the back of the theatre. Gertrude seems flushed, excited.

And Horatio joins Marcella and Ophelia near the front. Hamlet, taking the stage, makes a vague, anticipatory gesture.

QUEEN

Come hither, my dear Hamlet, sit by me.

HAMLET

No, good mother, here's metal more attractive.

He sits beside Ophelia, then seems to lose control of himself, sliding out of the chair onto her lap. Deadpan clowning.

POLONIUS
(*to Claudius*)

O, ho, do you mark that?

HAMLET

Lady, shall I lie in your lap?

He prises apart Ophelia's knees and rests his head in her lap. She's more than a little irritated.

OPHELIA

No, my lord.

Her voice is a sharp whisper. Hamlet whispers back.

HAMLET

I mean, my head upon your lap?

OPHELIA

Ay, my lord.

HAMLET

Do you think I meant country matters?

OPHELIA

I think nothing, my lord.

HAMLET

That's a fair thought to lie between maids' legs.

OPHELIA

What is, my lord?

HAMLET

Nothing.

OPHELIA

You are merry, my lord.

The lights dim.

67

Onscreen, video-projected colour bars appear, followed by a flickering countdown. Hamlet's voice rings out in the silence.

HAMLET

Who, I?

OPHELIA

Ay, my lord.

HAMLET

O God. What should a man do but be merry? For look you how cheerfully my mother looks, and my father died within's two hours.

A series of titles appear onscreen: THE MOUSETRAP / A TRAGEDY / BY HAMLET / PRINCE OF DENMARK

OPHELIA

Nay, 'tis twice two months, my lord.

HAMLET

So long? Nay then, let the devil wear black, for I'll have a suit of sables. O heavens! Die two months ago; and not forgotten yet? Then there's hope a great man's memory may outlive his life half a year. `

Claudius calls out to Hamlet, as if to cut him off.

KING

How fares our cousin Hamlet?

HAMLET

Excellent.

KING
(*turning to Polonius*)
Have you heard the argument? Is there no offence in it?

Polonius shrugs.

The video begins. An assemblage of found footage from other films. We see a rose blooming; an idyllic happy family: man and wife and a little boy. The earth spins calmly on its axis. All is well in the world.

Dissolve to: swarming microscopic cells. Then a quick cartoon shot of a hand pouring a bottle labelled with a skull and crossbones.

OPHELIA

What means this, my lord?

HAMLET

It means mischief.

Claudius's cell phone rings. He looks around, smiling apologetically as he shuts it off.

On the screen: an image of an ear as poison is poured into it.

Hamlet glares at Claudius.

Claudius looks at his watch, then back at the screen as a poisoned man clutches at his throat, convulsing.

Gertrude looks troubled. A tight smile forms on Claudius's face.

Hamlet looks at him – a clouded, excited look.

On screen: a soldier kisses the hand of a stately queen. Quick cut to an excerpt from a porno movie. Quick cut to a black tie audience, applauding. Cut to the apparent poisoner, a man facing himself in a mirror as he fits a crown on his own head.

Claudius stands, a bit unsteadily, and starts to clap. Gertrude looks at him, perplexed.

QUEEN

How fares my lord?

As if to apologize for his busy schedule, he gestures at his watch.

KING

Give me some light. Away!

POLONIUS

Lights, lights, lights!

Claudius rushes out, followed by Polonius. Gertrude flashes a look at Hamlet, then hurries to catch up with her husband.

HAMLET
O good Horatio, I'll take the ghost's word for a thousand pound. Didst perceive?

Horatio hesitates, then speaks coolly.

HORATIO
Very well, my lord.

HAMLET
Upon the poisoning?

HORATIO
I did very well note him.

Ophelia looks between them but Hamlet fails to register this, or Horatio's scepticism. He decisively turns on his heel, heading out of the room.

EXT. CITY STREET – NIGHT

Hamlet hails a cab.

HAMLET
(*voice-over*)

Some must watch, while some must sleep:
Thus runs the world away.

INT. CAB – NIGHT

Hamlet jumps in. He's about to slam the door when Rosencrantz and Guildenstern wedge their way in.

ROSENCRANTZ

Good my lord, vouchsafe me a word with you –

But the pre-recorded voice of Eartha Kitt interrupts:

EARTHA KITT
(*voice-over*)

This is Eartha Kitt. Cats have nine lives – *meoowrrr* – but unfortunately you have only one –

GUILDENSTERN
(*to Hamlet*)

The King, sir –

HAMLET

Ay, sir, what of him?

GUILDENSTERN

Is in his retirement marvellous distempered.

HAMLET

With drink, sir?

GUILDENSTERN

No, my lord, with choler.

HAMLET

Your wisdom should show itself more richer to signify this to the doctor, for, for me to put him to his purgation would perhaps plunge him into more choler.

GUILDENSTERN

Good my lord, put your discourse into some frame and start not so wildly from my affair.

HAMLET
I am tame, sir. Pronounce.

GUILDENSTERN
The Queen, your mother, in most great affliction of spirit,
hath sent me to you.

HAMLET
You are welcome.

GUILDENSTERN
Nay, good my lord, this courtesy is not of the right breed. If it
shall please you to make me a wholesome answer. I will do
your mother's commandment; if not, your pardon and my
return shall be the end of my business.

HAMLET
I cannot make you a wholesome answer; my wit's diseased.
[But, sir, such answer as I can make, you shall command, or
rather, as you say, my mother. My mother, you say –

ROSENCRANTZ
Then thus she says: your behaviour hath struck her into
amazement and admiration.

HAMLET
O wonderful son, that can so astonish a mother! But is there
no sequel at the heels of this mother's admiration? Impart.

ROSENCRANTZ
She desires to speak with you in her closet, ere you go to bed.

HAMLET
We shall obey, were she ten times our mother.]

*EXT. CHINATOWN STREET – NIGHT

*Hamlet strides down the sidewalk, in a rage, not mindful of the gun held
at his side.*

HAMLET
'Tis now the very witching time of night,
When churchyards yawn and hell itself breathes out
Contagion to this world. Now could I drink hot blood

And do such bitter business as the day
Would quake to look on . . .

*He wheels, steps into traffic, attempting to hail a cab. Cars whiz past.
After a moment he remembers the gun, pockets it, again waves for a cab.*

EXT. HOTEL ELSINORE – NIGHT

*Hamlet's cab coasts up; he hops out. He's heading in when he sees
Claudius in the lobby, conferring with his bodyguard.*

Hamlet backs up, crossing to Claudius's waiting limo.

*He raps on the glass, then opens the door, leans in and roughly tugs the
driver out of the car. He gives a harsh, whispered command, then slides
in behind the wheel.*

INT. HOTEL LOBBY – NIGHT

Claudius exits the hotel, passing a trick-or-treating ghost in a white sheet.

INT. LIMO – NIGHT

Claudius slides in, plucks a cell phone from its holster.

EXT. HOTEL – NIGHT

The limo pulls into the street, gliding like a shark.

INT. LIMO – NIGHT

Claudius is talking into the phone, his voice tight with rage.

KING

I like him not, nor stands it safe with us
To let his madness range. Therefore prepare you,
I your commission will forthwith dispatch,
And he to England shall along with you.

Hamlet, tensely driving, watches Claudius in the rear-view mirror.

The terms of our estate may not endure
Hazard so near's as doth hourly grow
Out of his brows.

GUILDENSTERN
(*over speaker*)

We will ourselves provide.
Most holy and religious fear it is
To keep those many many bodies safe
That live and feed upon Your Majesty.

Hamlet holds himself steady, steering through clotted mid-town traffic, but we can see agitation in his eyes.

Claudius flicks on the limo TV, channel surfing as Rosencrantz and Guildenstern hold forth. Soundless, turbulent images seem to illustrate his frenzied state of mind.

ROSENCRANTZ
(*over speaker*)

The single and peculiar life is bound
With all the strength and armour of the mind
To keep itself from noyance, but much more
That spirit upon whose weal depends and rests
The lives of many. The cess of majesty
Dies not alone, but like a gulf doth draw
What's near it with it.

GUILDENSTERN
(*over speaker*)

Never alone
Did the King sigh, but with a general groan.

KING

Arm you, I pray, to this speedy voyage,
For we will fetters put about this fear,
Which now goes too free-footed.

GUILDENSTERN
(*over speaker*)

We will haste us.

Claudius hangs up. He keeps his voice low and quiet, an internal voice.

KING

O, my offence is rank, it smells to heaven;
It has the primal eldest curse upon't,

A brother's murder. Pray can I not
Though inclination be as sharp as will.

The limo picks up speed. Hamlet staring at Claudius in the rear-view mirror.

My stronger guilt defeats my strong intent,
And like a man to double business bound
I stand in pause where I should first begin,
And both neglect.

Hamlet swerves to avoid a car; Claudius is jolted, and braces his spread hand over the TV. A stark silhouette. He keeps it there, as the limo settles.

What if this cursed hand
Were thicker than itself with brother's blood?
Is there not rain enough in the sweet heavens
To wash it white as snow?

Hamlet, reducing speed, reaches into his jacket, pulling out the gun.

Claudius, oblivious, remains crouched by the TV, its light flooding onto his face. As his thoughts bore in upon him, voice-over replaces actual speech.

(*voice-over*)
My fault is past, but O, what form of prayer
Can serve my turn?
(*he speaks aloud*)
'Forgive me my foul murder'?
(*back to voice-over*)
That cannot be, for I am still possessed
Of those effects for which I did the murder.
My crown, mine own ambition, and my queen.
May one be pardoned and retain th' offence?
In the corrupted currents of this world
Offence's gilded hand may shove by justice,
And oft 'tis seen the wicked prize itself
Buys out the law. But 'tis not so above.

He presses a button. The limo's overhead window slides back; skyscrapers float overhead.

There is no shuffling; there the action lies
In his true nature, and we ourselves compelled
Even to the teeth and forehead of our faults
To give in evidence. What then? What rests?
Try what repentance can. What can it not?

Hamlet fingers his gun, watching Claudius in the mirror. The limo slows.

                    HAMLET
                    (*voice-over*)
Now might I do it pat, now he is a-praying,
And now I'll do 't.

The limo comes to a halt in Times Square. The glare and flash of lights seem to heighten Hamlet's confusion. He turns and looks at Claudius, still kneeling before the TV, head lowered.

Hamlet raises his gun.

Claudius remains motionless, oblivious, head down.

                    KING
My words fly up, my thoughts remain below.
Words without thoughts never to heaven go.

Hamlet can't shoot. He turns, reaches for the door and runs out into the street.

We remain with Claudius, who looks up – squinting into the empty driver's compartment.

EXT. TIMES SQUARE – NIGHT

Claudius exits the limo. Electronically generated stock print-out streams overhead. He's back in his element, confident, self-possessed.

INT. KING AND QUEEN'S ROOM – NIGHT

Polonius urges Gertrude to have a sip from his drink, but she won't look up, her face obscured under a spill of hair.

POLONIUS

Look you lay home to him.
Tell him his pranks have been too broad to bear with,
And that your Grace hath screened and stood between
Much heat and him.

QUEEN

Fear me not.

A harsh knock on the door.

HAMLET

Mother, Mother!

Gertrude looks up. Polonius takes her by the arm, pulling her to her feet. She jerks away from him, but he looks at her squarely, as if to say: Snap out of it.

POLONIUS

I'll shroud me even here.
            (*he moves to the mirrored closet*)
Pray you, be round with him.

More banging at the door. Polonius hurries into the closet – then reappears, takes his coat, re-enters the closet, sliding the door shut behind him.

Gertrude makes her way to the door. As soon as she opens it, Hamlet enters, looking feverish, wild-eyed, striding back to the bedroom proper.

HAMLET

Now, Mother, what's the matter?

QUEEN

Hamlet, thou hast thy father much offended.

HAMLET

Mother, you have my father much offended.

QUEEN

Have you forgot me?

HAMLET

No, by the rood, not so.
You are the Queen, your husband's brother's wife,
And – would it were not so! – you are my mother.

QUEEN

Nay, then, I'll set those to you that can speak.

HAMLET

Come, come and sit you down.

He all but flings her onto the bed and, holding her jaw, forces her to look at herself in the mirrored closet. He's in a rage, all his frustration boiling over.

You shall not budge,
You go not till I set you up a glass
Where you may see the inmost part of you.

He shoves her against the closet so violently that she yells out.

QUEEN

What wilt thou do? Thou wilt not murder me? Help!

POLONIUS
(*yelling inside the closet*)

What ho! Help!

Hamlet fires the gun into the closet.

The mirror is abruptly spider-webbed with cracks.

Gertrude stares at the mirror (and at her own jagged reflection) in horror.

QUEEN

What hast thou done?

HAMLET

Nay I know not. Is it the king?

There's a clang of jostled clothes hangers, then the door opens and Polonius staggers out, one hand cupped over his eye. Blood is flowing beneath his hand.

Hamlet half catches him, but Polonius falls to the floor, dead.

QUEEN

O what a rash and bloody deed is this!

Hamlet kneels beside Polonius's body. The horror and finality of this act haven't quite hit him.

HAMLET

A bloody deed – almost as bad, good Mother,
As kill a king and marry with his brother.

QUEEN

As kill a king!

HAMLET

Ay, lady, it was my word.

Hamlet continues staring at the corpse, his eyes hard, remorseless.

Thou wretched, rash, intruding fool, farewell!
I took thee for thy better. Take thy fortune.
Thou find'st to be too busy is some danger.

He turns to Gertrude. She's stunned, silent, hysteria rising in her eyes.

Leave wringing of your hands. Peace, sit you down
And let me wring your heart, for so I shall,
If it be made of penetrable stuff.

QUEEN

What have I done?

[He sits beside her on the bed and takes her hands in his.

HAMLET

Such an act
That blurs the grace and blush of modesty,
Calls virtue hypocrite, takes off the rose
From the fair forehead of an innocent love,
And sets a blister there.

QUEEN

What act
That roars so loud and thunders in the index?

*[Hamlet grabs a photo of Claudius from the bedside table and prises
open his wallet, displaying a photograph of his father.*

HAMLET

Look here upon this picture –
This was your husband. Look you now what follows . . .
Here is your husband.

The Queen stares at the two pictures.]

Have you eyes?
You cannot call it love, for at your age
The heyday in the blood is tame, it's humble,
And waits upon the judgement.
Rebellious hell,
If thou canst mutine in a matron's bones,
To flaming youth let virtue be as wax
And melt in her own fire.

QUEEN

O Hamlet, speak no more.
Thou turn'st mine eyes into my very soul,
And there I see such black and grained spots
As will not leave their tinct.

In a rage, he starts tearing the sheets from the bed.

HAMLET

Nay, but to live
In the rank sweat of an enseamed bed,

Stewed in corruption, honeying and making love
Over the nasty sty –

QUEEN

O, speak to me no more.
These words like daggers enter in my ears.
No more!

HAMLET

A murderer and a villain,
A vice of kings,
A cutpurse of the empire and the rule,
That from a shelf the precious diadem stole
And put it in his pocket –

QUEEN

No more!

HAMLET

A king of shreds and patches –

A faint gust of smoke. Hamlet looks up to see his father's ghost, ruefully sitting on a chair by the bed, less than a foot away from Gertrude.

What would your gracious figure?

Gertrude looks where Hamlet directs the question – and sees nothing.

Hamlet half rises, staring at the ghost but still clutching his mother's wrist.

Do you not come your tardy son to chide.

QUEEN

Alas, he's mad.

GHOST

Do not forget. This visitation
Is but to whet thy almost blunted purpose.
But look, amazement on thy mother sits.
O, step between her and her fighting soul!

Hamlet redirects his attention to his mother.

Speak to her, Hamlet.

82

QUEEN

Whereon do you look?

HAMLET

How is it with you, lady?

QUEEN

Alas, how is't with you,
That you do bend your eye on vacancy,
And with th' incorporeal air do hold discourse?
O gentle son,
Upon the heat and flame of thy distemper
Sprinkle cool patience.
        (*but Hamlet is now looking again at the ghost*)
Whereon do you look?

HAMLET

On him, on him! Look you, how pale he glares!

The ghost, indeed, looks more than a little disgusted. His expression says: 'Calm down. Don't mess this up.'

– Do not look upon me.

The ghost rises and crosses to Polonius. He looks down at the corpse.

QUEEN

To whom do you speak this?

Hamlet's eyes swivel to track the ghost's invisible progress out of the room.

HAMLET

Why, look you there! Look how it steals away!
My father, in his habit as he lived!

QUEEN

This is the very coinage of your brain.
This bodiless creation ecstasy is very cunning in.

Hamlet stands.

HAMLET

Ecstasy?
My pulse as yours doth temporately keep time
And makes as healthful music. It is not madness
That I have uttered.

He turns back to Gertrude, with his former intensity and sharpness.

Mother, for love of grace,
Confess yourself to heaven,
Repent what's past, avoid what is to come;
And do not spread the compost on the weeds
To make them ranker.

GERTRUDE

O Hamlet, thou hast cleft my heart in twain.

HAMLET

O, throw away the worser part of it,
And live the purer with the other half.
Good night – but go not to my uncle's bed.
Assume a virtue if you have it not.
And when you are desirous to be blest,
I'll blessing beg of you. For this same lord –
                    (*indicating Polonius*)
I do repent, but heaven hath pleased it so,
To punish me with this, and this with me.

He kneels beside the body.

> I will bestow him, and will answer well
> The death I gave him.

INT. HOTEL BASEMENT — NIGHT

Hamlet lugs Polonius's body out of the elevator, dragging him by one foot. He pauses by a pay phone. Drops the corpse's ankle, fishes change from his pocket, picks up the receiver, taps in a number.

HAMLET
. . . One word more, good lady.

INT. KING AND QUEEN'S ROOM — NIGHT

Gertrude stands alone in the cold vast room. She's still shaken, stunned, trying to hold herself together. Her voice sounds lost.

Over the following, we INTERCUT between Gertrude and Hamlet on the phone.

QUEEN
What shall I do?

HAMLET
Not this, by no means, that I bid you do:
Let the bloat King tempt you again to bed,
Pinch wanton on your cheek, call you his mouse,
And let him, for a pair of reechy kisses,
Make you to ravel all this matter out,
That I essentially am not in madness,
But mad in craft.

This explanation, spoken with building bitterness and heat, makes him sound utterly mad.

QUEEN
Be thou assured, if words be made of breath
And breath of life, I have no life to breathe
What thou hast said to me.

HAMLET
I must to England; you know that.

85

QUEEN

Alack,
I had forgot. 'Tis so concluded on.

HAMLET

I'll lug the guts into the neighbour room.

Gertrude listens, in the silence, to her son's breath.

Mother, good night.

Hamlet hangs up. Then kneels again, almost tenderly, lifting Polonius's body into his arms.

He continues down the dark hall.

Indeed, this counselor
Is now most still, most secret, and most grave,
Who was in life a foolish prating knave.
Come, sir, to draw toward an end with you.
                    (*then, very quietly*)
Good night, mother.

*[EXT. HOTEL – NIGHT

Hamlet, alone now, strays into the street, fitting Walkman headphones to his ears. A cold raw wind hits his face, his clothes. On the soundtrack, a blast of Jimi Hendrix: 'Manic Depression'.

ANGLE ON WALL-MOUNTED HOTEL SURVEILANCE CAMERA

The camera stares after him.

EXT. SAMSUNG CONSTRUCTION SITE – NIGHT

Hamlet walks amidst swirling trash. He crosses the street, music still roaring.

He walks along a construction site. We glimpse him through windows cut into the provisional wooden barrier.

Hamlet doesn't see Rosencrantz and Guildenstern, who follow him from a safe distance. Guildenstern is fussing with an umbrella, which buckles in the wind – he drops it, and the thing skates away, tumbling end over end.]

EXT. FOUNTAIN – NIGHT

Hamlet moves toward the fountain, still wearing headphones, looking unhinged. He ascends the curving stairs.

He hovers on the upper landing, gazing down at the fountain, then turns – startled to see that Rosencrantz has followed him here.

ROSENCRANTZ
What have you done, my lord –?
> (*Hamlet removes his headphones*)
– with the dead body?

Hamlet is blank for a moment. Is he being followed everywhere? But he gathers himself together.

HAMLET
Compounded it with dust, whereto 'tis kin.

Rosencrantz fishes a cell phone from his pocket. He punches in numbers as Hamlet, glancing below, sees Guildenstern heading towards the stairs.

ROSENCRANTZ
Tell us where 'tis, that we may take it thence and bear it to the chapel.

Guildenstern reaches into his pocket as his cell phone rings.

HAMLET
Do not believe it.

ROSENCRANTZ
Believe what?

HAMLET
That I can keep your counsel and not mine own. Besides, to be demanded of a sponge, what replication should be made by the son of a king?

ROSENCRANTZ
Take you me for a sponge, my lord?

Hamlet starts walking away.

HAMLET
Ay sir, that soaks up the King's countenance, his awards, his authorities.

Rosencrantz catches up with him, handing over his cell phone; Hamlet holds it to his ear.

GUILDENSTERN
(*over phone*)
My lord, you must tell us where the body is and go with us to the King.

HAMLET
(*into phone*)
The body is with the King, but the King is not with the body. The King is a thing –

GUILDENSTERN
(*over phone*)
A thing, my lord?

Hamlet moves past Rosencrantz and drops the cell phone over the ledge – into the fountain below. Rosencrantz looks after the phone and

Hamlet strides past him, heading for a clear escape – only to run into
Claudius and two bodyguards as they emerge from the stairs. A wall of
implacable hostility.

Claudius looks grim, exhausted, but manages a tight smile.

> KING
>
> Now Hamlet, where's Polonius?

> HAMLET
>
> At supper.

The bodyguards move close.

> KING
>
> At supper? Where?

> HAMLET
>
> Not where he eats but where he is eaten. A certain convocation
> of politic worms are e'en at him. Your worm is your only
> emperor for diet. We fat all creatures else to fat us, and we fat
> ourselves for maggots. Your fat king and your lean beggar is but
> variable service – two dishes, but to one table, that's the end.

Rosencrantz and Guildenstern are now hovering near, and Claudius
steps closer, his patience wearing thin.

> KING
>
> Where is Polonius?

> HAMLET
>
> In heaven. Send thither to see. If your messenger find him
> not there, seek him i' th' other place yourself.

Claudius hauls off and slugs him in the gut. It takes a moment for
Hamlet to regain his breath.

> – But if indeed you find him not within this month, you shall
> nose him as you go up the stairs into the lobby.

> KING
> (*to Rosencrantz and Guildenstern*)
>
> Go seek him there.

HAMLET

He will stay till you come.

Rosencrantz and Guildenstern scurry off, and Claudius steers Hamlet to the waiting limo.

KING

Hamlet, this deed, for thine especial safety,
Which we do tender as we dearly grieve
For that which thou hast done, must send thee hence
With fiery quickness.
The bark is ready and the wind at help,
Th' associates tend, and everything is bent
For England.

Hamlet pauses, looking dazed.

HAMLET

For England.

KING

Ay, Hamlet.

HAMLET

Good.

KING

So is it, if thou knew'st our purposes.

HAMLET

Farewell, dear Mother.

KING

Thy loving father, Hamlet.

HAMLET

My mother – father and mother is man and wife, man and
wife is one flesh, and so, my mother.

*Hamlet kisses Claudius on the mouth. The older man recoils, then
regains control, guiding this problem child to the limo.*

EXT. LIMO/AIRPORT – NIGHT

The limo coasts up to the terminal.

*Hamlet gets out, heading for the terminal entrance as Rosencrantz and
Guildenstern scramble to gather luggage and Gertrude leaves the car,
eyes glittering, a drink in her hand.*

Mother and son embrace in the wind.

Claudius remains inside the limo, icily watching through the one-way glass.

KING

Away! For everything is sealed and done
That else leans on th' affair.
And England, if my love thou hold'st at aught –
As my great power thereof may give thee sense,
Since yet thy cicatrice looks raw and red
After the Danish sword, and thy free awe
Pays homage to us – thou mayst not coldly set
Our sovereign process, which imports at full
By letters congrueing to that effect
The present death of Hamlet. Do it, England,
For like the hectic in my blood he rages,
And thou must cure me.

INT. AIRPLANE, FIRST-CLASS CABIN – NIGHT

Hamlet, drinking whisky, has set up his Discman on his tray-table.

Across the aisle sit Rosencrantz and Guildenstern, sharing a copy of Wired *magazine with Fortinbras on the cover, and the caption: 'Fortinbras – moving into the millennium.'*

Hamlet pauses, then clicks off his Discman, staring at his in-flight TV monitor – a news broadcast showing Fortinbras's decisive exploits.

We see the young prince riding at the prow of a yacht, wind rippling through his hair and his Napoleon T-shirt. Then a flurry of corporate symbols. We can't hear the sound.

Hamlet flags down the flight captain.

> HAMLET
> (*indicating monitor*)
> Good sir, whose powers are these?

> CAPTAIN
> The nephew to old Norway, Fortinbras.

Rosencrantz and Guildenstern watch over the edge of their magazine as Hamlet unbuckles his seat belt, stands, slowly moves down the aisle.

The cabin is dark; nearly all the passengers are asleep, as if victims of mass hypnosis: a man in a sleep mask, his head flung back; a couple huddled together, holding hands.

> HAMLET
> How all occasions do inform against me
> And spur my dull revenge! What is a man,
> If his chief good and market of his time
> Be but to sleep and feed? A beast, no more.

Hamlet moves through a curtain, passes a dazed flight attendant, crossing into the crowded coach area.

> (*voice-over*)
> Sure he that made us with such large discourse,
> Looking before and after, gave us not
> That capability and godlike reason
> To fust in us unused. Now, whatever it be,

Bestial oblivion, or some craven scruple
Of thinking too precisely on th' event –
A thought which, quartered, hath but one part wisdom
And ever three parts coward – I do not know
Why yet I live to say 'This thing's to do',
Sith I have cause, and will, and strength, and means
To do't. Examples gross as earth exhort me –

He breaks off, arriving at a young boy, perhaps two years old, starting up from his mother's lap. The mother, pretty and young, is asleep, but the boy is awake, solemn and watchful.

Hamlet stares at him a moment, then turns back, slowly retracting his steps down the aisle.

INT. AIRPLANE LAVATORY – NIGHT

Hamlet enters the narrow, dim, low-ceilinged space. He scrutinizes himself in the mirror.

                    HAMLET
Rightly to be great
Is not to stir without great argument,
But greatly to find quarrel in a straw
When honour's at the stake. How stand I then,
That have a father killed, a mother stained,
Excitments of my reason and my blood,
And let all sleep. . . O from this time forth,
My thoughts be bloody, or be nothing worth!

FADE OUT.

FADE IN:

INT. GUGGENHELM MUSEUM – DAY

Claudius stares down from the upper ramp.

Ophelia drifts across a lower level, wild-eyed and lost.

Gertrude, on another ramp, looks radiant and calm amidst a crowd of well-dressed guests. Her attendant whispers into her ear.

QUEEN

I will not speak with her.

The attendant departs. Gertrude smiles, but we hear her inner voice.

(*voice-over*)
To my sick soul, as sin's true nature is,
Each joy seems prologue to some great amiss.
So full of artless jealousy is guilt,
It spills itself in fearing to be split.

Ophelia appears behind her.

OPHELIA

Where is the beauteous majesty of Denmark?

Gertrude starts backing away; Ophelia follows.

How should I your true love know
From another one?

QUEEN

Alas, sweet lady, what imports this song?

OPHELIA

Say you? Nay, pray you mark.

He is dead and gone, lady,
He is dead and gone;
At his head a grassgreen turf,
At his heels a stone.

QUEEN
Nay but Ophelia –

Gertrude arrives beside Claudius, who looks askance at Ophelia.

OPHELIA
Pray you mark.

QUEEN
Alas, look here, my lord –

KING
(*to Ophelia*)
How do you, pretty lady?

OPHELIA
Pray let's have no words of this; but when they ask you what it
means, say you this –

Ophelia screams.

In the lobby: partygoers look up, shocked and confused.

Gertrude, aided by Claudius's bodyguard, pulls Ophelia away.

*Gertrude rejoins Claudius as the bodyguard drags Ophelia down the
ramp.*

I hope all will be well. We must be patient, but I cannot
choose but weep, to think they would lay him i' the cold
ground. My brother shall know of it. And so I thank you for
your good counsel. Come, my coach! Good night, ladies,
good night, sweet ladies, good night, good night –!

Claudius and Gertrude retreat towards the elevator.

KING
How long has she been thus?

*Gertrude looks up as Laertes emerges from the elevator, charging
straight at them.*

QUEEN

Calmly, good Laertes.

LAERTES

That drop of blood that's calm proclaims me bastard,
Cries cuckold to my father, brands the harlot
Even here, between the chaste unsmirched brow
Of my true mother.

Laertes forces Claudius back toward a side gallery. Gertrude rushes after them.

INT. GUGGENHELM, BACK ROOM – DAY

Laertes barges in with Claudius, who remains imperiously calm.

KING

What is the cause, Laertes,
That thy rebellion looks so giantlike?

Gertrude tussles with Laertes, but Claudius restrains her.

Let him go. Do not fear our person.
There's such divinity doth hedge a king.

LAERTES

Where is my father?

KING

Dead.

QUEEN

But not by him.

KING

Let him demand his fill.

LAERTES

How came he dead? I'll not be juggled with.
To hell, allegiance! Vows, to the blackest devil!
Conscience and grace, to the profoundest pit!
I dare damnation. To this point I stand,
Let come what comes, only I'll be revenged
Most throughly for my father –

Who shall stay you?

LAERTES

My will, not all the world's.
And for my means, I'll husband them so well
They will go far with little.

*Claudius abruptly embraces Laertes, with an unexpected show of
emotion. Laertes freezes for a moment, then gives in to the embrace. He
looks bewildered, near tears.*

KING

Why, now you speak
Like a good child, and a true gentleman.
That I am guiltless for your father's death
And am most sensibly in grief for it.
It shall as level to your judgement 'pear,
As day does to your eye –

But now, past Claudius's shoulder, Laertes sees Ophelia.

*She reaches into her bag – and proceeds to scatter Polaroids torn from
her wall, pictures of flowers and leaves. She doesn't seem to know where
she is.*

OPHELIA

And will he not come again?
And will he not come again?
No, no, he is dead.
Go to thy death-bed.
He will never come again.

Laertes moves toward his sister.

LAERTES

Oh heat dry up my brains; tears seven times salt
Burn out the sense and virtue of mine eye!
By heaven, thy madness shall be paid with weight
Till our scale turn the beam. O rose of May!

Laertes puts an arm around her, protectively pulls her away.

Dear maid, kind sister, sweet Ophelia!

Hadst thou thy wits and didst persuade revenge,
It could not move thus.

She offers him a Polaroid.

OPHELIA

There's rosemary, that's for remembrance. Pray you,
love, remember.

*When Laertes refuses to take the photo, she lets it drop to the floor, then
offers another.*

And there is pansies, that's for thoughts.

*Claudius's bodyguard reappears, flanking Ophelia and Laertes as they
move to the door.*

There's fennel for you, and columbines.
There's rue for you, and here's some for me; we may
call it herb of grace o' Sundays. You must wear your rue
with a difference. There's a daisy. I would give you some
violets, but they withered all when my father died.
They say he made a good end –

*Gertrude kneels and picks up one of the fallen photos; Claudius stares
after brother and sister, his eyes hardening.*

[INT. MARCELLA'S APARTMENT – NIGHT

*A narrow railroad apartment. Marcella is pummelling a punching bag,
not far from Horatio tapping into a Powerbook.*

COMPUTER

Welcome. You've got mail!

Horatio squints at the monitor.

HORATIO

I do not know from what part of the world
I should be greeted, if not from Lord Hamlet.

*He clicks open the mail file, and quietly reads aloud, talking around a
cigarette.*

'Horatio . . . Let the King have the letters I have sent, and repair thou to me with as much speed as thou woulds't fly death . . . I have words to speak in thine ear will make thee dumb, yet are they much too light for the bore of the matter . . . Rosencrantz and Guildenstern hold their course for England. Of them I have much to tell thee . . . Farewell. He that thou knowest thine, Hamlet.'

INT. SQUAT – NIGHT

Ophelia flicks a zippo lighter and brings the flame to a Polaroid of Hamlet.

INT. SQUAT BATHROOM – NIGHT

Ophelia, nearly scorching herself, drops the flaming photo in the bathroom sink. As Hamlet's face crumples, glows, melts, we hear the medicine cabinet swing open and shut. Then we see Ophelia gulping down a handful of pills.

She glances at herself in the mirror, brushes hair from her face, then moves to the other room. We linger on the photo in the sink. The flame has died, leaving a blistered black square.]

INT. THE KING AND QUEEN'S BEDROOM – NIGHT

Claudius stands over the blood-stained rug, facing himself in a cracked mirror – the detached closet door, banked against the bedroom wall. A hotel handyman is installing a new unbroken door while another hotel employee measures the closet threshold with a beeping, laser-activated device.

                         KING
                    (*voice-over*)
     Where th'offence is, let the great axe fall.

The doorbell buzzes – Claudius turns, crossing to the front room. He passes Gertrude, who stares after him, a question clouding her eyes.

INT. FRONT ROOM, THE KING AND QUEEN'S SUITE – NIGHT

Claudius's bodyguard opens the door, revealing Laertes. He's changed clothes and shaved and looks re-assembled, self-possessed.

Claudius leads Laertes into the front room, clapping him on the shoulder with a strong paternal air.

KING

Now must your conscience my acquittance seal
And you must put me in your heart for friend,
Sith you heard –

Claudius opens a desk drawer and brings out a plastic evidence bag containing the gun Hamlet used on Polonius.

That he which hath your noble father slain
Pursued my life.

Laertes stares at the bag, then glances up as the two hotel men walk out with the door, reflections sliding across the broken mirror.

LAERTES

It well appears.
                    (*the hotel men exit*)
But tell me
Why you proceeded not against these feats
So crimeful and capital in nature,
As by your safety, wisdom, all things else,
You mainly were stirred up.

Claudius moves to the bedroom threshold, hovers a moment, then turns back to Laertes. He proceeds to fix drinks, keeping his voice low.

KING

The Queen his mother
Lives almost by his looks, and for myself –
My virtue or my plague, be it either which –
She is so conjunctive to my life and soul,
That, as the star moves not but in his sphere,
I could not but by her.

LAERTES

And so have I a noble father lost,
A sister driven into desperate terms.
Whose worth, if praises may be back again,
Stood challenger on mount of all the age
For her perfections. But my revenge will come.

Claudius hands him a drink, sits beside him.

KING

Break not your sleeps for that. You must not think
That we are made of stuff so flat and dull
That we can let our beard be shook with danger
And think it pastime. You shortly shall hear more.
I loved your father, and we love ourself,
And that, I hope, will reach you to imagine –

*The fax machine starts to whirr – and spits out a single page. Claudius
swiftly stands, takes it, reads to himself.*

– From Hamlet.
Laertes, you shall hear:
                    (*reading*)
'High and mighty, you shall know I am set naked on your
kingdom. Tomorrow shall I beg leave to see your kingly eyes,
when I shall, first asking your pardon, recount the occasion of
my sudden and more strange return.
Hamlet.'

He looks at Laertes, then back at the fax.

'Naked'.

LAERTES

Let him come.
It warms the very sickness in my heart
That I shall live and tell him to his teeth,
'Thus diest thou'.

Claudius steps near. A new edge in his voice.

KING

If he be now returned, I will work him
To an exploit now ripe in my device,
Under the which he shall not choose but fall;
And for his death no wind of blame shall breathe,
But even his mother shall uncharge the practice
And call it accident.

*The phone rings. Claudius tenses. On the third trill, Gertrude picks it up
in the bedroom. Laertes moves to the window; Claudius follows.*

Laertes, was your father dear to you?
Or are you like the painting of a sorrow,
A face without a heart?

LAERTES

Why ask you this?

KING

There lives within the very flame of love
A kind of wick or snuff that will abate it,
And nothing is at a like goodness still,
For goodness, growing to a pleurisy,
Dies i' his own too much. That we would do
We should do when we would, for this 'would' changes,
And hath abatements and delays as many
As there are tongues, are hands, are accidents,
And then this 'should' is like a spendthrift sigh,
That hurts by easing. But, to the quick o' th' ulcer –
Hamlet comes back. What would you undertake
To show yourself your father's son in deed
More than in words?

*He hands Laertes the plastic-sheathed gun. Laertes considers it a
moment, then returns it as Gertrude emerges from the bedroom. Her
face is shadowed until she moves into the light. She looks shocked,
shattered.*

QUEEN

One woe doth tread upon another's heel,
So fast they follow: Your sister's drowned, Laertes.

LAERTES

Drowned!

EXT. FOUNTAIN – NIGHT

*Camera approaches the upper railing, then moves past it, discovering
Ophelia's body in the fountain below. Her weighted bookbag seems to be
holding her in place; the red box and little rubber duck bob beside her
outspread hair.*

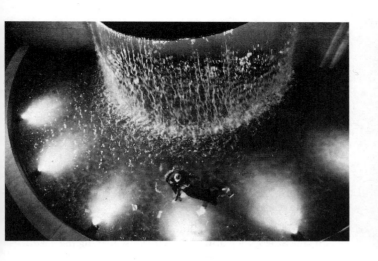

QUEEN
(voice-over)

Drowned, drowned . . .

A cop splashes into the fountain, fumbling and lifting the dead girl.

Hamlet's letters remain floating in the bright blue water.

FADE OUT.

FADE IN:

EXT. AIRPORT – DAY

Hamlet emerges through reflective sliding glass doors. He catches something in his hands – a red motorcycle helmet.

Horatio, who has just tossed it to him, steps forward and they embrace.

EXT. HIGHWAY – DAY

Hamlet rides behind Horatio on Horatio's motorcycle. skimming past airport signs, a descending jet.

EXT. GRAVEYARD – DAY

Among the stones and crypts, kids are playing in Halloween outfits. They scatter as Horatio's bike rounds a bend, slowing alongside an embankment

Over this we hear the grinding sound of a backhoe, and the gravedigger's voice, a gravelly growl, singing.

> GRAVEDIGGER
> (*off-screen*)
> 'There must be some way out of here,'
> Said the joker to the thief.

The Gravedigger is young, close to Hamlet's age. The backhoe, operated by another man, finishes clawing at the earth. The Gravedigger moves to the grave, shovelling out broken roots.

> 'There's too much confusion, I can't get no relief.
> Businessmen, they drink my wine, plowmen dig my earth,
> None of them along the line know what any of it is worth.'

Hamlet and Horatio dismount the bike and remove their helmets.

[The Gravedigger, seeing them approach, chooses to ignore them.

> 'No reason to get excited', the thief he kindly spoke,
> 'There are many here among us who feel that life is but a joke.
> But you and I, we've been through that, and this is not our
>   fate –

Hamlet comes forward, oddly cheerful among the markers and stones.

> HAMLET
> Whose grave's this, sirrah?

> GRAVEDIGGER
> Mine, sir.

He hardly glances up, keeps humming the song.

> HORATIO
> I think it be thine indeed, for thou liest in't.

> GRAVEDIGGER
> You lie out on't, sir, and therefore 'tis not yours. For my part,
> I do not lie in't, yet it is mine.

HAMLET
Thou dost lie in 't, to be in't and say it is thine. 'Tis for the dead, not for the quick, therefore thou liest.

GRAVEDIGGER
'Tis a quick lie sir, 'twill away again from me to you.

The gravedigger proceeds to gather up his belongings: a lunch box and thermos.

HAMLET
What man dost thou dig it for?

GRAVEDIGGER
For no man, sir.

HAMLET
What woman, then?

GRAVEDIGGER
For none neither.

HAMLET
Who is to be buried in't?

GRAVEDIGGER
One that was a woman, sir, but, rest her soul, she's dead.

HAMLET
How long hast thou been a gravemaker?

GRAVEDIGGER
Of all the days i' the year, I come to't that day that young Hamlet was born – he that is mad and sent into England.

HAMLET
Ay, marry, why was he sent into England?

GRAVEDIGGER
Why, because he was mad. He shall recover his wits there, or if he do not, 'tis no great matter there.

HAMLET
Why?

GRAVEDIGGER

'Twill not be seen in him there. There the men are as mad as he.

HAMLET

How came he mad?

GRAVEDIGGER

Very strangely, they say.

He looks Hamlet in the eye as he says it; then, as if abashed, he moves away, tidying up. He finds and folds a dirty wedding veil, left behind by the playing kids.

HAMLET

How long will a man lie i' th' earth ere he rot?

GRAVEDIGGER

Faith, if he be not rotten before he die – as we have many pocky corpses nowadays, that will scarce hold the laying in – he will last you some eight year or nine year.

He returns to the grave, pokes at something with his toe.

Here's a skull now hath lien you i' th' earth three-and-twenty years.

Hamlet kneels a moment, then stands up into frame wearing a rubber Halloween skull mask. He puts on a creepy, mock-scary voice.

HAMLET

Horatio, tell me one thing.

HORATIO

What's that, my lord?

HAMLET

Does thou think Alexander looked o' this fashion i' the earth?

HORATIO

E'en so.

Hamlet takes off the mask.

HAMLET

And smelt so? Pah!

HORATIO

E'en so, my lord.

HAMLET

But soft . . .

Hamlet drops the mask. We hear singing from close by. Young voices making their way through a hymn.]

Hamlet moves with Horatio towards the source of the singing. They ascend the embankment. Camera reveals a funeral in progress, two dozen young people gathered around a casket. Conspicuous among the mourners are Laertes, Claudius, his bodyguard, Gertrude, her attendant and a Priest.

The King, the Queen, the courtiers. Who is this they follow?
And with such maimed rites!

HORATIO

This doth betoken
The corpse they follow did with desperate hand
Fordo its own life. 'Twas of some estate.

HAMLET

Ophelia . . .

Horatio nods.

ANGLE ON OPHELIA'S GRAVE

The hymn is over. Everyone looks shell-shocked. Laertes approaches the Priest.

LAERTES

What ceremony else?

PRIEST

Our obsequies have been as far enlarged
As we have warranty. Her death was doubtful,
And but that great command o'ersways the order
She should in ground unsanctified have lodged
Till the last trumpet.

LAERTES

Must there no more be done?

PRIEST

No more be done.

LAERTES

Lay her i' the earth,
And from her fair and unpolluted flesh
May violets spring! I tell thee, churlish priest,
A ministering angel shall my sister be
When thou liest howling.

Hamlet moves forward with Horatio as Gertrude scatters flowers over the grave.

QUEEN

I thought thy bride-bed to have decked, sweet maid,
And not have strewed thy grave.

LAERTES

O treble woe
Fall ten times treble on that cursed head
Whose wicked deed thy most ingenious sense
Deprived thee of! Hold off the earth a while,
Till I have caught her once more in mine arms.

III

Claudius grabs his arm but Laertes breaks free and jumps into the grave.

> Now pile your dust upon the quick and dead,
> Till of this flat a mountain you have made.

Hamlet steps closer, in torment.

HAMLET

What is he whose grief
Bears such an emphasis, whose phrase of sorrow
Conjures the wand'ring stars and makes them stand
Like wonder-wounded hearers?

*Everyone freezes, horrified, astonished. Hamlet extends his hand –
Laertes takes it, stepping out of the grave.*

LAERTES

The devil take thy soul!

Laertes strides away; Hamlet follows.

HAMLET

I loved Ophelia. Forty thousand brothers
Could not, with all their quantity of love
Make up my sum. What wilt thou do for her?
Show me what thou't do, I'll do it.
Woo't weep, woo't fight, woo't fast, woo't tear thyself?
Woo't drink up eisel, eat a crocodile?
I'll do it. Dost come here to whine?

*Laertes snaps, wheels, lunges at him. They tumble to the ground.
Claudius and Gertrude start after them.*

ANOTHER ANGLE

*as Hamlet and Laertes skid, grapple and slide down the slope dividing
two crypts.*

KING

Pluck them asunder.

QUEEN

Hamlet, Hamlet!

Laertes lunges and grabs Hamlet by the throat, applying pressure – but he abruptly breaks off, devastated, ashamed. Hamlet thrashes out from under him, gasping.

HAMLET
What is the reason that you use me thus?
I loved you ever. But it is no matter.

The King, Queen and attendants arrive at the embankment's crest.

Hamlet stands, and we hear Horatio's motorcycle coasting up.

Let Hercules himself do what he may,
The cat will mew, the dog will have his day.

EXT. HIGHWAY – DUSK

Hamlet rides behind Horatio as the city rises from the road's curve, preceeded by a miniature city of multiple billboards.

INT. MARCELLA'S APARTMENT – DUSK

Marcella lies asleep in bed. The ghost of Hamlet's father is sitting beside her, grave and sympathetic, as if sharing her troubled dream.

The ghost looks up as the door opens – Hamlet talking as Horatio leads him in.

HAMLET
In my heart there was a kind of fighting
That would not let me sleep –

Indicating the sleeping girl in back, Horatio gestures for Hamlet to be quiet. Apparently neither of them sees the ghost. Hamlet lowers his voice but keeps talking as Horatio moves into the kitchen area.

Rashly,
And praised be rashness for it – let us know,
Our indiscretion sometimes serves us well
When our deep plots do pall, and that should learn us
There's a divinity that shapes our ends,
Rough-hew them how we will –

INT. PLANE, FIRST-CLASS CABIN – NIGHT (FLASHBACK)

Hamlet stands from his seat. His lowered voice narrates ensuing action.

> HAMLET
> (*voice-over*)
> Up from my cabin, in the dark . . .

He hovers over Rosencrantz (in a sleep mask) and Guildenstern, asleep in their seats, Rosencrantz's head resting on his friend's shoulder.

Hamlet reaches into the overhead compartment, pulls down a computer case.

> (*voice-over*)
> Groped I to find out them, had my desire,
> Fingered their packet, and in fine withdrew
> To mine own room again –

He brings the case to his own seat. Unzips the laptop computer. Boots it up. His eyes narrow as he scrolls through files.

> (*voice-over*)
> – making so bold,
> My fears forgetting manners, to unseal
> Their grand commision; where I found, Horatio –
> Ah, royal knavery – an exact command:
> My head should be struck off . . .

INT. MARCELLA'S APARTMENT – AFTERNOON

Hamlet stands before Horatio, offering a red floppy disk.

> HORATIO
> Is't possible?

> HAMLET
> Here's the commision. Read it at more leisure.
> But wilt thou hear now how I did proceed?

> HORATIO
> I beseech you.

INT. AIRPLANE, FIRST-CLASS CABIN – NIGHT (FLASHBACK)

Hamlet, accessing the King's document, proceeds to revise the text.

> HAMLET
> (*voice-over*)
> Being thus benetted round with villainies – I sat me down,
> Devised a new commission, wrote it fair . . .

CLOSE ON THE MONITOR

as Hamlet replaces his name with those of Rosencrantz and Guildenstern.

> (*voice-over*)
> An earnest conjuration from the King,
> That on the view and knowing of these contents,
> Without debatement further more or less,
> He should these bearers put to sudden death.

INT. MARCELLA'S APARTMENT – NIGHT

Horatio looks startled. Then a kind of hard fatalism takes hold in his eyes.

> HORATIO
> So Guildenstern and Rosencrantz go to't.

Hamlet sees that his friend is shaken. He moves closer, insistent.

> HAMLET
> Why, man, they did make love to this employment.
> They are not near my conscience; their defeat
> Does by their own insinuation grow.
> 'Tis dangerous when the baser nature comes
> Between the pass and fell incensed points
> Of mighty opposites.
> Does it not, think thee, stand me now upon –
> He that hath killed my king and whored my mother,
> Popped in between the election and my hopes
> – is't not perfect conscience
> To quit him with this arm? And is't not to be damned
> To let this canker of our nature come
> In further evil?

Hamlet's voice has woken Marcella, who sleepily shuffles into the room, receives a kiss on the forehead from Horatio, then continues into the kitchen. Horatio glances after her, then back to Hamlet.

HORATIO

It must be shortly known to him from England
What is the issue of the business there.

HAMLET

It will be short. The interim's mine.
And a man's life's no more than to say 'one'.

Horatio sits beside Marcella; Hamlet moves closer.

But I am very sorry, good Horatio,
That to Laertes I forgot myself.
For by the image of my cause I see
The portraiture of his –

The trill and whirr of a fax machine. They all freeze, watching the fax paper slide out – the cover sheet on Denmark corporate stationery. Horatio takes the paper from the machine.

HORATIO

The King, sir.

> *(he reads to himself; then)*

The King hath wagered that in a dozen passes between yourself and Laertes, he shall not exceed you three hits. He hath laid on twelve for nine, and it would come to immediate trial, if your lordship would vouchsafe the answer.

A pause. Horatio passes the fax to Hamlet.

HAMLET

How if I answer no?

Horatio shrugs, plainly sceptical.

If it please his Majesty, it is the breathing time of day with me.

But Horatio looks wary, worried.

HORATIO

You will lose, my lord.

HAMLET

I do not think so.

(a pause)

But thou wouldst not think how ill all's here about my heart; but it is no matter.

HORATIO

If your mind dislike anything, obey it. I will forestall their repair hither, and say you are not fit.

Hamlet looks between Marcella and Horatio, and a deep lucid calm overtakes him.

HAMLET

Not a whit, we defy augury. There is special providence in the fall of a sparrow. If it be now, 'tis not to come; if it be not to come, it will be now; if it be not now, yet it will come. The readiness is all. Since no man owes of aught he leaves, what is't to leave betimes?

Hamlet glances up – and sees his father standing beside the refrigerator. Their eyes meet. Hamlet is reconciled, unafraid.

Let be.

INT. KING AND QUEEN'S HOTEL ROOM – NIGHT

A hand crushes a white powder over a glass of wine. As the powder dissolves into the liquid, we hear Claudius's quiet voice.

KING

Hamlet, this pearl is thine.

He raises the glass in a toast.

Here's to thy health.

INT. HAMLET'S BACK ROOM – NIGHT

Hamlet removes photos and cards collaged on his wall.

He pauses a moment, lingering on a shadowy snapshot of Ophelia. Then he peels it off the wall, lets it drop, looks up.

Horatio has arrived at the room's threshold.

Hamlet joins him, gives the room one last look, then flicks off the lights.

EXT. HOTEL ELSINORE – NIGHT

The city is aglow, lights bleeding through heavy mist.

EXT. ROOF – NIGHT

Gertrude sits tense and expectant in a thronelike chair, close by a collection of onlookers – attendants, friends, photo-journalists. Horatio, Marcella and Bernardo are also here.

> HAMLET
> Give me your pardon, sir. I have done you wrong –

The terrace has been re-configured into a provisional fencing arena. Laertes and Hamlet stand facing each other on a narrow metal strip. They're wearing formal fencing garb – close-fitting white outfits with electronic 'tails', wires which travel up to an overhead pulley system, linking them to a touch-sensitive scoring system and to each other.

> – But pardon 't, as you are a gentleman.
> This presence knows, and you must needs have heard
> How I am punished with a sore distraction.
> What I have done,
> That might your nature, honour, and exception
> Roughly awake, I here proclaim was madness.

Laertes looks unconvinced.

> Sir, in this audience
> Let my disclaiming from a purposed evil
> Free me so far in your most generous thoughts
> That I have shot an arrow o'er the house
> And hurt my brother.

Laertes, flint-eyed, turns to Osric, the referee.

> LAERTES
> Give us the foils. Come on.

*Osric is a tall, sad-eyed, older man. He presents a case of duelling swords.

HAMLET

I'll be your foil, Laertes. In mine ignorance
Your skill shall, like a star i' the darkest night,
Stick fiery off indeed.

Laertes selects a sword, then testingly slashes the air with it, displaying impressive agility and skill.

LAERTES

You mock me, sir.

HAMLET

No, by this hand.

KING

Cousin Hamlet, you know the wager?

HAMLET

Very well, my lord.
Your grace has laid the odds on th' weaker side.

Following Laertes's lead, Hamlet fits a fencing helmet to his head.

KING

I do not fear it. I have seen you both.
But since he is bettered, we have therefore odds.

LAERTES

This is too heavy. Let me see another.

HAMLET

This likes me well. These foils have all a length?

OSRIC

Ay, my good lord.

Laertes selects another sword. And his eyes, meeting the King's, set off a spark of anxiety in the older man.

Osric steps back as they prepare to go at it, and the king steps forward.

KING

Set me the stoups of wine upon that table.
Give me the cups,
And let the kettle to the trumpet speak,

The trumpet to the cannoneer without,
The cannons to the heaven, the heaven to earth,
'Now the king drinks to Hamlet'.

Cups are set out on a little table. Hamlet removes his helmet for a moment, giving a last look to Horatio, Marcella, Gertrude. Then he refits the helmet to his head, turns to Laertes.

HAMLET

Come on, sir.

LAERTES

Come, my lord.

With unexpected decisiveness, Hamlet advances and lunges, striking Laertes in the chest.

The scoring panel buzzes and lights up.

HAMLET

One.

Laertes stares at him, vacantly.

LAERTES

No.

Hamlet looks at him, half smiling at the absurdity of this denial. He turns to Osric.

HAMLET

Judgement.

OSRIC

A hit, a very palpable hit.

LAERTES

Well, again.

KING

Stay, give me drink.

Claudius reaches for the cup of wine then, as if in afterthought, turns to Gertrude, gesturing at Hamlet.

Give him the cup.

HAMLET
I'll play this bout first. Set it by awhile.

*Claudius sets down the cup. Gertrude looks between the cup and
Claudius, suspicion blooming in her eyes.*

*Hamlet and Laertes resume the match. Laertes remains stiff and blank
but Hamlet, attempting to lighten things up, executes some spoofy Kung
Fu moves. Laertes just stares at him.*

As if chastened, Hamlet advances and deftly darts in, scoring another hit.

The scoring panel buzzes and lights up.

Another hit, what say you?

LAERTES
A touch, a touch. I do confess't.

Claudius turns to the queen.

KING
Our son shall win.

Gertrude stands, flushed, and walks toward Hamlet.

QUEEN
Here, Hamlet, take my napkin, rub thy brows.
The queen carouses to thy fortune –

She veers and grabs the cup from Claudius's hand. There's an angry lucidity in her face.

My lord, I pray you pardon me.

She quickly drinks from the cup. Claudius, staring in horror, has nothing to say.

(*to Hamlet*)
Come, let me wipe thy face.

Hamlet regards her with impatience, but relents. They embrace, and he gives her a look of quick, conflicted tenderness before turning back to Laertes.

HAMLET
Come, for the third, Laertes. You do but dally.
I pray you, pass with your best violence.

Laertes has left the fencing strip, and is rummaging through his gym bag.

LAERTES
Say you so? Come on.

Laertes pulls a gun from the bag – the same gun Hamlet used on Polonius. He strides forward and fires. The bullet strikes Hamlet in the chest.

Have at you now!

Another shot. It's not clear whether Hamlet has been hit again. He charges at Laertes. They scuffle, fall, thrash on the ground. Laertes drops the gun and tries to strangle Hamlet with his suit's electronic cord. Hamlet gags, gropes – and his hand finds the gun.

KING
Part them, they are incensed.

Hamlet brings the gun muzzle to Laertes' ribcage.

Nay, come – again!

He shoots. Osric and Horatio rush forward to separate them.

Gertrude takes a few steps, then wavers, looking lost.

OSRIC

Look at the queen there, ho!

Osric's voice is a hoarse whisper. Everyone seems to freeze, staring at Gertrude as she ventures into the duelling area, moving towards Hamlet.

Laertes tries to stand but his legs buckle – he falls to the floor, clutching his stomach, the white suit soaked with blood.

LAERTES

I am justly killed with mine own treachery.

Gertrude sways; Claudius is moving unsteadily towards her, but she collapses into Hamlet's arms. He half cradles and carries her, lowers her into a chair.

KING

She swoons to see them bleed.

Hamlet holds Gertrude's hand, strokes her hair, but she's staring straight ahead – at the ghost of Hamlet's father. The ghost stares back, an ache in his eyes.

QUEEN

No, no, the drink, the drink – O my dear Hamlet – the drink, the drink! I am poisoned.

Hamlet can't see what she sees. He gets to his feet.

HAMLET

O villainy! Treachery. Seek it out.

LAERTES

It is here, Hamlet.

Hamlet wheels around, dizzy, the world crashing inside his head. He stumbles into Osric.

LAERTES

The foul practice hath turned itself on me.

*The gun is still in Hamlet's hand. He stares at it almost tenderly.
Assembled spectators are scared, cowering under the threat of further
violence. Marcella has moved to Gertrude, checking her pulse.*

Lo, here I lie,
Never to rise again. Thy mother's poisoned.
I can no more. The King, the King's to blame.

*Claudius turns to Hamlet, a worried smile on his face, his hands
outstretched – a gesture of surrender or supplication.*

But Hamlet lifts the gun and fires.

*Claudius clatters and falls back into empty chairs. He tries to stand, to
climb up into a chair. The chair topples and spins.*

KING

O yet defend me, friends! I am but hurt.

*But he's bleeding badly, lying even as he dies, blood issuing from his
mouth.*

Hamlet takes the cup of poisoned wine.

HAMLET

Here, thou incestuous, murderous, damned Dane. Drink of
this potion. Follow my mother.

*He tries to pour and pump the wine into the King's mouth. But
Claudius is dead.*

Hamlet looks up and sees his father.

LAERTES

Exchange forgiveness with me, noble Hamlet.
Mine and my father's death come not upon thee,
Nor thine on me!

He dies. Hamlet, staring at his father's ghost, hardly seems to notice.

HAMLET

Heaven make thee free of it! I follow thee.

Horatio lowers Hamlet into the King's thronelike chair.

HAMLET
I am dead, Horatio. Wretched Queen, adieu!
You that look pale and tremble at this chance,
That are but mutes or audience to this act –

Horatio crouches beside Hamlet, trying to hold him together.

Had I but time – as this fell sergeant, Death,
Is strict in his arrest – O, I could tell you –
But let it be. Horatio, I am dead;
Thou livest; report me and my cause aright
To the unsatisfied.

A spasm passes through his body. But Hamlet masters it, staring up at Horatio with hard clear eyes.

If thou didst ever hold me in thy heart,
Absent thee from felicity awhile,
And in this harsh world draw thy breath in pain,
To tell my story.

Marcella joins Horatio; as he turns to her, Hamlet, still holding the gun, raises it to his temple. CLICK! The chamber is empty. CLICK!

– The rest is silence.

He lowers his hand as Horatio, horrified, takes the gun.

Hamlet is dead. Horatio closes his staring eyes.

HORATIO
Now cracks a noble heart. Good night, sweet prince,
And flights of angels sing thee to thy rest . . .

*[EXT. DENMARK CORPORATION – NIGHT

Smoke seethes from the building's tall roof. We hear sirens, and the increasing, throbbing noise of an approaching helicopter.

EXT. HOTEL ELSINORE – NIGHT

Wind from the arriving chopper sweeps across the blood-soaked terrace. And a retinue of men – Secret Service types in dark suits – scurries

*forward, the wind at their backs. Followed by a scruffy young man
wearing a sharp suit, a hat with earflaps, a bag slung on one shoulder.
Fortinbras.*

*Fortinbras stands fast in the wind, surveying the scattered corpses with a
cold, disdainful eye.*

He spots Horatio as helicopter noise and wind die down.

FORTINBRAS

Where is this sight?

HORATIO

What is it you would see?
If aught of woe or wonder, cease your search.

FORTINBRAS

This quarry cries on havoc. O proud Death,
What feast is toward in thine eternal cell,
That thou so many princes at a shot
So bloodily hast struck?

Horatio turns to Osric.

HORATIO

Give order that these bodies
High on a stage be placed to the view,
And let me speak to the yet unknowing world
How these things came about. So shall you hear
Of carnal, bloody, and unnatural acts,
Of accidental judgements, casual slaughters,
Of deaths put on by cunning and forced cause,
And, in this upshot, purposes mistook
Fall'n on th' inventors' heads. All this can I
Truly deliver.

Fortinbras reaches into his bag, pulling out a digital video camera.

FORTINBRAS

Take up the bodies. Such a sight as this
Becomes the field, but here shows much amiss.

He clicks on the camera.

VIDEO POV

Scattered bodies, carnage. Desolate and stark as any crime scene. Horatio and Marcella tend to Hamlet's body. Osric moves to the queen.

Fortinbras steps past Claudius, tracking bloody prints as he stands on the King's chair for a better view.

He turns and faces the remaining witnesses, spectators, survivors.

Then Fortinbras swivels around, aiming his camera straight into ours. He mutters to himself.

Go, bid the soldiers shoot.

QUICK FADE TO BLACK

THE END]

APPENDIX I
An Inventory of Ghosts (*Hamlet* on Film)

'There is no mystery in a looking glass until someone
looks into it.'

    – Harold Goddard, *The Meaning of Shakespeare*

It was eye-opening to sift through some of the earliest, silent
*Hamlet*s – fragments, many of them, images convulsing under
strobe-like effusions of chemical decomposition. I cut in a few
seconds' worth of an Italian version, circa 1910, during the film
within the film, before learning that the BFI's price for the footage
was unaffordable. At any rate, these films brought home the fact
that, even with the text preposterously amputated, *Hamlet* is a play
loaded with resonant pictures.

But the cinematic ground zero for this adaptation was Olivier's
shadow-filled 1948 version, a virtual *film noir* featuring swooping
crane shots and radical cuts (Rosencrantz and Guildenstern were
not simply dead, they were expunged, Fortinbras never showed
up, and Hamlet's 'How all occasions do inform against me . . .'
soliloquy was dropped when the director/star determined he didn't
look right wearing 'a ridiculous tam-o'-shanter hat'). I remember
feeling, on first exposure to it, that the film leaned too heavily on
melodrama, on a forced reading of the Prince as a character
possessing one fatal flaw ('This is the story of a man who could
not make up his mind') and Olivier's performance, for which he
won an Academy Award, seemed somewhat archaic, masklike,
self-satisfied. But, now that I'm out of high school, these first
impressions have dissolved; the movie seems charged with
conviction and excitement, the screenplay a model of astute
streamlining, and Olivier's portrayal strikingly detailed and
complete. More to the point for the work at hand, I noticed that
Olivier was particularly smart about applying purely cinematic
interludes to pace and balance dense stretches of language. His
camera prowls Elsinore's corridors, winds up coiling stairs, and
lingers on Ophelia (a radiant Jean Simmons) in life and death.
The result is an atmosphere of fearful watchfulness, in which

silence, shadows, music and camera movement heighten the text.

At any rate, Olivier's *Hamlet*, upon its debut, seemed so definitive that no other incarnations were attempted on film for some fifteen years – a lull followed by an outpouring of *Hamlets* which continues to this day. 1964 saw *three* estimable productions: Grigori Kozintsev's Russian film, with a text translated by Pasternak, a score by Shostakovich, and an impressively glowering Inokenti Smokhtunovski in the title role; John Gielgud's documentation of his modern-dress staging, with Richard Burton as Hamlet, Eileen Herlie reprising the role of Gertrude (she'd played opposite Olivier sixteen years earlier) and Gielgud, off camera, as the Ghost; and Philip Saville's *Hamlet at Elsinore*, a BBC production with a notably strong (and young) cast: Christopher Plummer as Hamlet, Robert Shaw as Claudius, Michael Caine as Horatio, Donald Sutherland as Fortinbras.

I look forward to someday seeing a fabled spaghetti western, *Johnny Hamlet*, produced by Sergio Leone in 1968, but this, at the time of my research, escaped my view. Of conspicuous ensuing interpretations – Tony Richardson's with Nicol Williamson (1969), Franco Zeffirelli's Mel Gibson vehicle (1990), a PBS production catching Kevin Kline's run at New York's Public Theatre (1990) and Kenneth Branagh's unexpurgated, all-star treatment (1996) – I'd single out Nicol Williamson's performance as particularly riveting. (No one, it seems to me, has matched Williamson's depiction of lacerating intelligence.)

Readers interested in tracing the play's full cinematic lineage would do well to track down Bernice W. Kliman's meticulous, multi-faceted study: *Hamlet: Film, Television and Audio Performance* (1988; currently out-of-print and ripe for revision). But the ghosts of past Hamlets that truly haunted my thinking tended to be more obscure, eccentric and non-English. Aki Kaurismaki's *Hamlet Goes Business* (1987) features a hilariously morose, mock-heroic treatment in which Hamlet, a bratty would-be businessman, turns out to have poisoned his own father. The movie – black and white, in Finnish – opens with the pasty-faced Prince stuffing his face with a fistful of ham. Uncle Claudius is a natty, mustachioed smoothie intent on overtaking the world market for rubber ducks. Ophelia, a fairly frumpy girl, gulps pills and drowns in her bathtub while playing a beloved pop song. Most of the updatings and

transpositions have this quality of smirky inanity, and
Shakespeare's text is trashed or ignored, but Kaurismaki manages
to capture the mournful, corrosive core at the heart of Hamlet's
psyche. The film deserves to be better known.

The same can be said for Kurosawa's 1961 *Hamlet*-derived *The
Bad Sleep Well*. Kurosawa set his story in a corrupt corporate
world and applied a number of the play's plot coordinates: an
avenging son, a questionable ghost, poison, an atmosphere of
escalating paranoia. Despite a great, eerie score and a fierce
performance from Toshiro Mifune, it's one of Kurosawa's more
uneven films, oddly unfocused, but it refuses the stamp of high-
minded hope with which Kurosawa often concluded his stories,
and this gives it something extra, a poignant element of trauma,
pitching Shakespeare's scepticism within a distinctly un-
Elizabethan view of the world as a dingy, destructable place.

Andrei Tarkovsky exerted another distant but essential
influence, by way of his posthumously published notes on *Hamlet*,
written in preparation for a stage production mounted in the late
seventies. 'She deliberately drinks the wine,' Tarkovsky wrote of
Gertrude's decision to take the fatal glass. I accepted this as a
conclusive blessing, having already considered the idea, which
Diane Venora, a veteran of the play, embraced. Tarkovsky's notes
also confirmed a conviction that the ghost of Hamlet's father
should be presented as a solid presence rather than a spectral
special effect – ghosts, for many of us, being as real as anyone in
our lives. The handkerchief carried by Sam Shepard, staunching
fluids leaking from his poisoned ear, was Tarkovsky's idea.

Lastly, this distinctly American, millennial *Hamlet* owes a good
deal to an octogenarian Swede. I watched a tape of Ingmar
Bergman's stage production of *Hamlet*, performed in Swedish at
the Brooklyn Academy of Music in 1990. I watched it twice.
Hamlet was played with virtuosic agility by Peter Stormare (best
known on these shores for his appearance in Coen Brothers
movies), the action unfolded with minimal scene design and
props, and Bergman's great skill in compressing and clarifying the
drama made the play feel new. The director took the liberty, now
and then, of bringing key characters – Ophelia and the Ghost,
mostly – into scenes where they were traditionally uninvited. But
these and other inventions felt motivated, scrupulous and

meaningful. Even on video, captured with a halting single camera, the result was spellbinding. A high-water mark to which this current production stumblingly aspired.

APPENDIX II
Director's Notes

page 5

The bracketed lobby and basement scenes were shot and edited into the movie. They weren't half bad. But it became apparent that the Elizabethan language, coming thick and fast at the outset, confused our early audiences. (A test screening organized by Miramax yielded the second worst scores in the company's history.) More to the point, it was troublingly clear that Hamlet's first appearance in the film came too late and felt flat.

Admitting that we needed a more urgent start, Ethan and I sat down with a pixel camera and worked out a new introduction, a video diary excerpt from one of our favourite speeches (a scene we had botched, midway through the shoot, in the presence of a full crew, the ever-patient pair of Steve Zahn and Dechen Thurman, and a leaky rain-making machine).

I held the camera while Ethan adjusted lights, fooled with a water glass, executed a rudimentary conjuring trick. We were alone in a hotel room, between setups during a weekend's worth of pickup shots. Hamlet's glorious speech was stripped down to this:

I have of late, for reasons I know not, lost all my mirth . . .

What a piece of work is a man?
How noble in reason, how infinite in faculties, in form how like an angel, in apprehension how like a god, the beauty of the world, the paragon of animals . . .

And yet to me, what is this quintessence of dust . . . ?

Backed by a cross-mix of Morcheeba and orchestral music by Niels Gade (an authentic Dane) and intercut with images I'd shot off the TV during the bombing in Bosnia, this 'improvised' scene now kickstarts the movie, giving the Prince a series of intimate close-ups and a private (pixelated) language. The idea was to frame and foreground Shakespeare's words, trusting them to bring an audience closer. The lobby scene with Bernardo, Horatio and

Marcella was accordingly collapsed, folded into a flashback when Hamlet's friends report the first ghost sighting.

page 16

In my memory, we were constantly behind schedule, re-shuffling scenes, dropping shots. We were routinely stalled in traffic, admiring massive lighting rigs mounted for the latest efforts of Martin Scorsese and Spike Lee. We had time – cast and crew alike – to speculate on how great it'd be if we had more time. The actors, lugging their famous lines into unlikely locations, were valiant and patient and under enormous pressure, their work often crowded by my preoccupation with camera angles and the DP's compulsion to light protectively, anticipating the fall-off in picture quality incurred by the blow-up from 16 to 35mm.

And so Hamlet's first soliloquy was restricted to his hotel room, as we never managed to shoot the more active material, flash cuts intended to open out the scene. In fact, as we rushed through the shoot, invented interstitial material was often delayed or dropped. Early on, however, I managed to enlist Jem Cohen to roam around town with me for a couple days, equipped with a tripod and a rented Bolex. From this we harvested a half-dozen crucial shots featuring jet trails, statues, turreted skyscrapers, a baleful urban waterfall. What's the point of these images, apart from simple punctuation? Something to do with architecture and mortality, time travel, ghosts. New Yorkers, Jem might tell you, are surrounded at every turn by radiant ephemera, ruins and things that will outlast us – distinctions that begin to blur if your view happens to be filtered through (and transformed by) a camera.

page 40

The bracketed Polonius material was adjusted the day of the shoot largely because we hadn't managed to wrangle Bill Murray into posing for Ophelia's photos, a key ingredient in justifying his presence in the scene. So I came up with the tenuous idea that it was Ophelia's birthday! So the set decorator ran out for cake boxes and balloons. And we staged the scene so that Polonius wearily treads upstairs and finds his daughter with the guy he had expressly forbidden her to see. An improvement on the script since it allowed Bill to underline what he was going for throughout his performance, portraying Polonius as a confounded father, a man who displaces every tender impulse toward his children with a cross-cancelling need to control them.

page 49

These cab/bicycle scenes were sacrificed when we ran behind schedule. And, straining to find the film's structure, we concluded that the 'To be or not to be . . .' soliloquy would play best in this spot, following Hamlet's first failure to kill Claudius.

This scene – cited by more than a few critics as if it were the adaptation's defining conceit, the most audacious thing in the movie – was intended to be split between three locations. Bill Viola granted us permission to film his spectacular video installation, 'Slowly Turning Narrative', while his retrospective was on view in the Whitney Museum. The piece seemed almost ready-made as a mirror for Hamlet's state of mind, for Shakespeare's hypnotic words. The idea was to then balance the Viola video with its nemesis, a Blockbuster store with mass-market images flooding in from the store's monitors.

But Ethan Hawke's impromptu marriage to Uma Thurman scotched our plans to shoot Bill's piece before the exhibition moved to Amsterdam. For months, I nursed the delusion that we could still haul Ethan and a skeleton crew across the ocean to finally 'complete' the scene – it seemed that important to include an example of video imagery so searching and rich, and I was slow to realize that the lonely Blockbuster aisles, with their in-house 'Action' signs and 'Go Home Happy!' wall placards, just might be sufficient.

page 65

Julia Stiles, at seventeen, had an uncanny ability to intimidate almost everyone on the set. Her calm seriousness, a sense of unbudgeable inner gravity, could be beautifully unsettling. One of my sharpest peripheral memories of her is very simple: Julia crouched on the floor, facing a particular bend of the wall in the Guggenheim Museum, her head lowered under Walkman headphones, her arms crossed. It was four or five in the morning; I was feeling particularly useless; the crew was clattering away.

When the camera was ready Julia quietly removed her headphones, stood and moved into frame, and in the guise of 'acting' some desperate grieving part of herself came swimming up in her eyes.

Days later, we shot the scene in which Ophelia burns Hamlet's photo and pops pills, one long take. We cut it in, abridged, while Hamlet's 'Get thee to a nunnery' speech plays on Ophelia's answering machine. The earlier business – Ophelia destroying the machine – was also shot but replaced with the above. A little on-screen madness goes a long way.

page 72

It seemed like a fair idea to throw Hamlet, Rosencrantz and Guildenstern into Chinatown, to admit more local reality into the movie, and so a sequence of eventually excised scenes had Hamlet running through Chinatown streets, pursued by his disloyal friends. He ducks into a particular nerve-jangling video parlour; R & G catch up with him in a dingy back room. This is the 'Play the pipe' scene, with Hamlet passing his gun – the 'pipe' – to Guildenstern, then scornfully taking it back.

> . . . There is much music, excellent voice, in this little organ, yet cannot you make it speak. 'Sblood, do you think I am easier to be played on than a pipe? Call me what instrument you will, though you can fret me, you cannot play upon me.

An envelope filled with cash bought us about twenty minutes with a horde of oblivious teenage video addicts and their thrilling, deafening, death-filled games. (More disassociated images-within-images! Sleepwalkers! Enemies of consciousness! Contemporary Rosencrantzes & Guildensterns!) Earlier, on the streets, we were shooting from an open van without permits or lights ('running and gunning', in AD lingo), when the absurdity of what we were up to fully kicked in. On the neon-lit sidewalk, standing in a crush of pedestrian traffic, amidst a sea of Asian faces, Ethan was recognized – by Gwyneth Paltrow, strolling along with Ben Affleck. Dechen, Steve and I stood by as introductions were made (Ethan and Ben had never met) and pleasantries exchanged. 'How's the baby? What are you up to?' 'We're doing *Hamlet*.' 'Oh, I heard about that. When are you doing it?' 'Now,'

Ethan said, '*Right now*. There's the camera. This is it!'

For the back room scene, on a separate night, the art department threw together an impressively desolate three-walled set, replete with a live rooster rented for the occasion. (Until fairly recently, a tic-tac-toe playing rooster, electrically motivated, had been one of the arcade's featured attractions. The caged bird, pacing across a soiled newspaper photo of Fortinbras, is one of my favourite missing images in the film.) My friend Yun-Fei gamely pitched in, exhorting Hamlet with Shakespearean dialogue translated into Chinese.

But, despite energetic work from actors and non-actors alike, the resulting scenes weren't half as cohesive as I'd hoped. They were somehow too busy, they clotted the film's forward motion, they weren't *necessary*. Alas.

page 87

The Mayor's Office listed at least forty other films shooting in Manhattan while *Hamlet* was up and running, and we had dire, ongoing trouble securing locations. It was especially difficult, on our budget, to find and lock high-end corporate spaces. Permissions were vaguely 'pending', or denied, or granted then revoked, as if to highlight the capricious nature of the heavily healthy stock market that made the city look at once prosperous and in the process of being dismantled. It turned out that shooting an active construction site was all but impossible, and other potentially nifty ideas proved impractical or out of reach.

And so, despite rigorous preparation, there was a steadily growing element of tension, even desperation, attending our days and nights, and Ethan became particularly vocal in letting me know that my ingenuity in staging scenes was threatening to overwhelm his ability to perform them.

He was right. The 'Where's Polonius?' scene, preserved here as first conceived, was a case in point. (Actually the first, even more intricate, conception had the action staged in the zooming capsule-shaped elevators of the Times Square Marriott, before the management flatly denied us access.) At any rate, a last-minute sidestep carried us from the fountain where Ophelia soon drowns to a laundromat (I was still thinking about water), where we shot without fear of traffic, wind or pedestrians shouting non-Shakespearean epithets. (Thanks to Anthony Katagas, for hooking us up with his uncle's place in Queens.)

page 106
I think it was Harold Goddard who pointed out that no character in the play can match Hamlet when it comes to verbal sparring, no one is his intellectual equal – except the nameless Clown (as he's designated in the text) digging Ophelia's grave in this famously mordant wild-card of a scene. I liked the idea of the gravedigger being a kind of uncrowned prince and purposely cast the part young, tagging Jeffrey Wright, a dazzling actor, expert at conveying wiley intelligence. We shot in a vast cemetery, Halloween day, autumn leaves flickering in the sun. Jeffrey was primed; the scene seemed to fly. But in the editing room it became clear that I'd failed to get it right. The tone and timing were off, and the whole episode seemed to sidetrack Hamlet's response to Ophelia's death. The movie worked better with the prized scene cut out. But we kept a vestige of Jeffrey's performance, a chorus from the Dylan song, as a wistful souvenir.

page 119
The referee in a fencing match is officially called a 'director', and in illustrating this esoteric pun I cast Paul Bartel in the role of Osric. I can be counted among the many enduring fans of Paul's *Death Race 2000*, and years ago he fell asleep on my couch (Amy Hobby recently reminded me; I'd forgotten) when a fellow film-maker brought him along to watch a rare blues documentary on tape. Paul showed up for work on *Hamlet* wearing his own spiffy clothes. (He also came with a remarkably tall stack of Sam Shepard first editions, which their author gamely signed.) He was the oldest person on the set, and arguably the most patient. Though he was typecast in films as a particular breed of snob, a supercilious would-be aristocrat, there was nothing arrogant about him, and nothing of the bitter, begrudging aspect I've come to dread in older directors. In fact, throughout our long nights together on a mid-town rooftop, forty-eight storeys up – despite the cold, the wind, the intermittent drizzle, and the threat of multiple nervous breakdowns from assorted colleagues – he never complained. He seemed permanently amused. It now occurs to

me that the farcical aspect of the shoot resembled nothing so much as one of his own movies.

News of his death came as a shock. He'd called a few weeks earlier to let me know he liked *Hamlet* – the film listed in newspaper obituaries as his last screen appearance. As we spoke, there was no intimation that he was ill, nothing to shadow his hopeful talk about a future that, it turned out, didn't exist for him. I hardly knew him, but I felt – still feel – a kind of distilled familiarity from watching his best work, *Death Race 2000* and *Eating Raoul* and his brilliant first film, *The Secret Cinema* – sly sharp movies, embracing a world of mayhem and malice while managing to remain, like Paul himself, essentially sweet-natured.

page 127
A large part of the brilliance, the completeness, of Shakespeare's ending for *Hamlet* lies in the ways in which principal characters, facing death, are each allowed a final, defining moment. They reach out, or shrink into themselves, as if obeying some imperative at the core of their natures. Laertes exchanges forgiveness with Hamlet, expressing a generosity he displays nowhere else. Gertrude (knowingly or not) takes poison and sacrifices herself for her son. Claudius, mortally wounded, his treachery revealed at last, launches a final selfish lie – 'Assist me, friends, I am but hurt!' And Hamlet, after chasing his thoughts in scene after scene of astonishing language, arrives at a place past which language cannot go: 'The rest is silence.'

But silence doesn't spill over onto the other characters, which further proves the play's scope. Horatio offers a concluding declaration of selflessness; the English Ambassador expresses less convincing dismay, then crassly, officially ups the body count ('Rosencrantz and Guildenstern are dead. Where should we have our thanks?'); then Fortinbras shows up.

Who is Fortinbras? Jan Kott makes a point of declaring that every production of *Hamlet* virtually defines itself by the treatment of the Norwegian prince, glimpsed and mentioned throughout the play but given precious little to say until he finally takes the stage in the last scene, confronting Hamlet's corpse.

Ethan and I spent a good deal of time talking about Fortinbras. I made a case for the character as a kind of doppelgänger, a proud, fatherless prince, like Hamlet, but deprived of Hamlet's melancholy, his self-loathing, his talent for introspection. Fortinbras is decisive and active, a warrior, a winner. He's also an embodiment of history – history's bloody bootprint, stamping remorselessly among the corpses of all overcomplicated young men, the ones who hesitate, who stun themselves looking into mirrors, the poets, the losers.

Ethan was pretty good at resisting this. It sounded too abstract to him, and we had trouble agreeing on who to cast in the role. It's curious, now, after all that talk, to see how Fortinbras's presence in the film became so fragmentary, nearly anonymous, as befits a prince in the age of faceless corporate power. All the same, as the movie took shape in the editing room, the characterization felt like a real failure. But then, sifting through the rooftop footage, it'd be unfair to single out one particular disaster. Did I mention that things went wrong? The cold, the rain, the sense of furious disappointment? The roof had been dressed by the art department with a steel fencing strip, a jerry-rigged bungee cord pulley system, and an array of chairs. The effect was so unimpressive that our expert fencing consultants – two impatient, inky-haired brothers in their twenties – suspected that we were mocking the art of fencing and contrived an excuse to abandon the project, taking their equipment with them. (The electronic scoring device you see in the movie was eventually rented from an aficionado in New Jersey, months later, and is visible only in close-ups.) After that drama unravelled, there were other displays of pique, trouble with squibs (the explosive charges that splatter fake blood when prop guns are fired), evidence of pride, insecurity, hysteria and fatigue. There was also, I rush to add, plenty of angelic behaviour and some terrifically focused acting. (Top prize, I don't mind telling you, goes to Karl Geary, who played Horatio with unrivalled compassion.)

In any case, my storyboards proved useless. and it was impossible to pretend that we were doing justice to the fine-meshed intricacy of Shakespeare's ending. By the time Fortinbras arrived, by (off-screen) helicopter, as the script ambitiously described, the wind machines simulating chopper wash were both feeble and deafening, and the extras recruited for the scene were uniquely wooden. Picture, if you will, a bedraggled film crew on a freezing, corpse-cluttered roof, wind machines roaring, Casey Affleck looking like he'd just arrived from the set of another movie (he had, in fact, flown in from Texas) and the sun coming up fast . . .

Everyone's confidence was jolted by an awareness that this was pretty surely not the best way to end the movie. Throughout the shoot we made other recognizable mistakes, but none so damaging to morale or to the film's ultimate meaning. After an early pass, I was discouraged enough to step way back, uncharacteristically allowing Kris Boden to work through the scene without me. She patiently carved the footage to the bone. (David Ray, sitting in while Kris was on another film, contributed his refining touch.)

And still, up to the last weeks of editing, Ethan and I were determined to re-think and re-shoot the scene. But our friends at Miramax – busily dreaming up alternative titles for the film – were unwilling to throw us more money, and Casey Affleck was unavailable for further shooting – a blessing in disguise, as it turned out. The last-ditch solution (sparked by Lois Smith) involved transposing Fortinbras's lines to another corporate mouthpiece, a newscaster, making Hamlet's replacement more cruelly anonymous. Robert MacNeil, formerly of the MacNeil/ Leher News Hour, was lured out of retirement (his wonderful memoir, *Wordstruck*, reveals a deep love of Shakespeare) and additional lines were lifted from the Player King's speech, sagely quoted in Harold Bloom's *Shakespeare, the Invention of the Human*.

> Our wills and fates do so contrary run
> That our devices still are overthrown;
> Our thoughts are ours; their ends none of our own.

Professor Bloom starts his book with these lines, and makes a convincing case for their centrality in Shakespeare's sceptical long view of things. When Mr MacNeil suggested we feed him the text on a teleprompter, it made perfect sense to end this image-saturated movie with a final shot of – *words*. Shakespeare's words, ascending a glowing screen. Safe to say they'll survive a deluge of further adaptations, images and ideas, until silence swallows us all.